At the
Manger

The Stories of Those

Who Were There

At the
Manger

The Stories of Those
Who Were There

Peter Vance Orullian

descant publishing

Descant Publishing
PO Box 12973
Mill Creek, WA 98208

Manufactured in the United States of America

1 3 5 7 9 10 8 6 4 2

Library of Congress Control Number: 2001118901

ISBN: 0-9712909-0-3

Interior Illustrations by Katie Garner.
Dust jacket design by Peter Orullian & Anderson Business Graphics.

Visit: www.atthemanger.com

For Cathryn,
who makes living a beautiful thing
to write about,
and who taught me more about
the child in the manger . . .
than anyone.

Acknowledgments

When I set out to write this book, I hadn't anticipated my great fortune to meet so many kind, intelligent, generous people along the way. But without these good folks, you wouldn't be holding this gentle artifact right now. So it is that I take great pleasure in pointing fingers and naming names.

Thank you, Ephraim and Virginia Orullian. Here is a book you can "get behind." Your support and patience with me as parents is legendary to those who know me. For your superb example of charity, service and sacrifice, I am eternally grateful. These qualities informed me in the telling of these tales.

To Star Orullian, for your practical disinterest in the business side of my preparations, and for saying "yes" almost before you knew what I meant to ask of you; and for teaching me to sing Christmas carols in the basement when we cuddled close as kids. To Todd and Julie, for a cautiousness that made me think even harder. And to the rest of Ephraim's children for allowing me to haul you into the Rocky Mountains, build a fire, and make you listen to the stories that fell from my pen.

Then there is Jay Davis. Thanks, friend, for your careful eye and your publishing wisdom—even the stuff I ignored. Mostly, though, thanks for being you. With you yoked to the team, I had less to carry.

My gratitude to Lizzy Shannon and Lenora Good, for insight and polish that gave context and color to this fictional world. And to Katie Garner, who rendered the images herein.

Special thanks to Bill Johnson, a master story analyst and delightful conversationalist.

For accuracy in the details I acknowledge Dr. Winthrop Lindsay Adams, Associate Professor of History, University of Utah; and Dr. Scott Noegel, Department of Near Eastern Languages & Civilizations, University of Washington.

For quick response time and unyielding honesty, Alan and Ezzie Anderson must take a bow, as must Larry Carpenter for taking a leap of faith on me without a contract.

And thanks to James Pace for an invitation to write. I'm blessed to know you.

No Christmas book of mine comes into the world without a big salute to Albert Finney and James Stewart, who remind me all year long to make good choices, Christmas choices. Nor is this page of thanks complete without a nod to Mr. Charles Dickens, both for his fine Christmas stories and his wonderful authorial voice.

And I'll thank just one song. That's right, "Greensleeves!" Legend has it that King Henry VIII wrote it for Anne Boleyn during their courtship around 1530, but there is no substantial evidence to back this up. The tune, with the original lyrics, first appeared in 1652, but the melody is thought to have originated in the late 1500s. After the American Civil War, William Chatterton Dix used the melody to write the popular Christmas Carol, "What Child is This?" More than any other song, this one stirs my soul.

My profound appreciation always to Cathryn, for reading, listening, hoping, and for caring about the Yuletide season almost as much as I do.

Finally, to the child who came and influenced a world. I do you the honor I can with my little pen. Thank you for being my dearest, finest friend.

Table of Contents

Author's Note - xiii

The Manger Part I - 1

The Handmaiden - 13

Twice a Gift - 31

A Night of Peace - 45

A Potter's Clay - 61

Swaddling Clothes - 75

The Rugmaker - 93

The Watchman - 115

The One - 133

The Beggar - 149

Olive Branch - 165

Father's Vineyard - 183

The Manger Part II - 201

Author's Note

A few years ago, a dear friend, laden with the responsibility of planning a Christmas celebration, asked me to pen a few stories to be read at his party and thus break the monotony of typical Yuletide festivities. For this one particular party amongst the slew of such celebrations that fill our holidays, he wanted something unique, something to call attention to the meaning of the season.

Undaunted, as every young writer must be, I wrote three stories in three days: soliloquies of two men and a woman who lived in Bethlehem and stood witness to the Birth of Jesus Christ. I intended for my stories to be given as first-person narratives, the actors and actress to dress the parts and deliver meaningful readings of my words.

And that's just what happened.

Then, people began to request copies of the tales, and the idea burgeoned to create many more stories, and expand those I had already written.

But perhaps this book starts further back than this.

As a boy, I looked forward to the tradition in our home of rescuing the Christmas decorations from their dusty basement cupboards. This day always came on December 4th, my sister Star's birthday. Star was named such because, being born in December, Dad considered her his Christmas star. We ate authentic Armenian food, then set to transforming the house. As always, I battled my little sister for the honor of setting up the Nativity. Most often, we did it together, leading to my purchase of Greg Olsen's print depicting just such a scene.

Anyway, I delighted in taking perfect care in the placement of those figurines. As a child, I believed in the personification of any- and everything: from piano legs, to heat-vents, to inanimate Nativity figures. I simply knew that these small bits of ceramic had stories to tell. After everyone was in bed, I sat in front of the Nativity, watching blinking Christmas tree lights reflect in the blank screen of our television, and gazing up at the single yellow globe that lit the straw and manger in aureate hues. And often I believed I could hear that night so long ago echoing forward in time. Or maybe everything is one eternal breath, and attentive as I was, I was able to partake of it in those silent moments of our front room.

Today, a host of travelers wend their way in my mind, making journeys begun in the stillness of my imagination. I follow along, interested to see where they lead me, grateful that I may witness their grand stories. And when the time is right, I'll put their journeys down on paper, just as I've done here. For they are as real to me as anything I know. Perhaps because I learn from them, perhaps because I want to believe in the worlds they inhabit.

In this world of Bethlehem as I have imagined it, there lives a carpenter, Luke, with the quandary of performing free work when he is in desperate need of money. His story is partially given to begin the book, and weaves its way through each of the other tales, concluding at the book's end. As so often happens in our lives today, interdependency grows between the characters of the stories, and Luke's life touches them all in unique ways, though every story may be read and enjoyed independently.

Where words and terminology of the time of Jesus did not perfectly translate, I've adopted terms that today's reader will understand. But in an effort to create a flavor of authenticity, I have left others, using the biblical term Yahweh for God, and Jeshua for Jesus.

These stories are dear to me because they speak to what I like best about Christmas, indeed what I believe Christmas is all about: giving of one's self. The story and life of Jesus Christ is such a story. And I live in the thought that his humble birth was a touchstone for others to offer that which was best within themselves.

As their stories echo forward in time, I hope they do the same for you.

> Merry Christmas,
> Peter Orullian

At the
Manger

The Stories of Those

Who Were There

The Manger ~ Part 1

knew if I did not find work, I
might lose her. Not to starvation, but by losing her respect, which is
the same as death. Worse still, if I could not find a way to earn money,
we might lose our unborn child. I'd not worked in months;
tradesmen barked for jobs at every turn, but good work could not be
found. Ruth and I had sold most of our finer things to purchase food.
Bitterness and anger entered my heart. How could I provide for Ruth?
For our child? I desperately pleaded with God to touch the hearts of
those I called upon for work to offer me a contract. But the months
passed and my tools lay dormant as I watched our home grow
barren and my wife grow thin.

One morning Ruth came home with a lightsome step, singing a tune, and kissed me on the forehead. "Be happy, Luke, all is well."

I stared at her dubiously. The lack of food had gone to her head.

"Don't look at me so, my love. Our prayers have been answered. I have found you a job." She spoke evenly, attempting to disguise her enthusiasm as though it was just another natural thing.

I jumped from my chair, knocking it over in my rush. "Work!"

"Oh, yes, something I think. Are you interested?" She began to busy herself in preparing supper, maintaining an oblivious attitude to my eagerness.

"Tell me, woman! I am going mad!" I took her hands and pulled her close to force an answer.

She ended her charade of casualness and smiled her glorious, everything-is-going-to-be-all-right smile. "Oh, Luke, it is a blessing. Michael Bar-jebus, the innkeeper, has agreed to have you construct some items for his stable. If he is pleased with your work, he will commission you for all his current needs."

My hands seemed to drop of their own volition. I hated to look at Ruth's broad smile with such disdain, but this did not seem to me to be good news. "I am to build for him for free, and then he will decide whether or not to use my services?" My voice grew caustic, stealing the hope from Ruth's lips.

"Luke, please. It is a chance for months of work. All you have to do is—"

"All I have to do is work for free! How do you suppose I will afford the materials to do this?" I demanded, having become the inquisitor. I paced, the heat in my face burning beneath my skin and causing the onset of a headache.

"We will manage," Ruth said quietly. "What else should we do?"

I pivoted on my heel and threw up my arms. "Tell him to take his magnanimity and carry it to Egypt! Suppose he does not like what I build? Suppose he only wants some free labor and stable construction? What if he is using us and has no intention of giving me paying work? No respected carpenter works for free. To do so would set a dreadful precedent. Other tradesmen will shut me out if they hear of it."

"The others will take the job if you do not, my love." She watched me earnestly. "I believe Michael is as good as his word, if a little awkward at times. He can be trusted to meet his obligations."

I narrowed an angry gaze at Ruth, feeling incriminations in her words. "And I do not, is that what you mean to say?" I stepped toward her. "Your husband, the carpenter, is not equal to the task of providing for *his* wife and unborn child, meeting *his* obligations. Well, perhaps you'd like to wed the innkeeper, play nursemaid to a crowd of vagrants and ruffians? Is that an obligation you'd like to keep?" I glowered.

"Luke, I only—"

"You only want to make a mockery of my covenant to keep you in good stead. You'd have me groveling at the feet of other men, abasing myself like a slave or beggar. Worse, you do it *for* me. What kind of man must he think I am, sending my wife to ask for work, then bargaining to do it for free? How can I show my face to him now, even if he has honest work for me? I'll end up apologizing for being so desperate? He'll feel magnanimous giving me work he doesn't even have to pay for. Is this the opportunity you speak of, Ruth? Is this the blessing?"

Ruth cowered before my objections. She fled our home and left me to mill in my own suspicion and frustration and anger. I knew she was right, and I did want to trust that all would be well. But there was little to encourage me—everyone seemed to be cutting expenses to make tax payment by census. Homes did not rise with the same frequency as even a year ago. The repairs of my own home had been stalled. But it would not be a home at all if these difficulties of the world drove a wedge between my wife and me. That would be no place to bring a child . . . A moment later I went after Ruth.

The following day I paid the innkeeper a visit. I resented having to go at all. I felt like a child again, asked to perform a chore, putting my expertise to use for free. I was a craftsman, yet my skill held only enough value to audition for work? It took all my patience to hold my tongue as Michael and I toured his inn. We looked at his personal living quarters, the common room, and the stables. After reviewing everything, he turned a blank look to me. He seemed to possess the ability to make me feel unworthy of working for him, though it may well have been my own discomfort that I was feeling. He had an intimidating brow, and I had the feeling he knew how desperately I needed the work.

I considered what needed to be done. Ruth had been right. The inn badly needed repair. Several months worth of work if we reached an agreement. Michael wanted another shed for storage, tables and chairs were mentioned as we had passed through the common room, and the stables needed to be firmed up, among other things. All the work involved a great many days of labor. Casting my eyes around, I fastened on a simple idea. "I see you simply throw your feed on the ground for the animals to eat as they can. You could use a manger or two for the donkeys your patrons stable here. Of course, there is much to be done in the inn itself, but I could have a feedbox done in a day or so." I swallowed my pride, and asked, "Would that be sufficient to demonstrate my abilities for you?"

He rubbed the corner of his eye with a dirty finger, a burp rumbling simultaneously out of him. His face scrunched up as though he had eaten something sour. He considered my offer as he looked around the stable, seeming to take stock of whether he had any real need for a manger. Finally, he pursed his lips and drummed a finger over them. Then he nodded.

"Fine. I will be back in a few days with a manger." I walked quickly away before he could decide that he wanted more of me. Besides, proposing work done for free humiliated me, especially when my wife needed food and other household items.

I meandered slowly home, muttering to myself. Passing an alley of food merchants where my fellow tradesman often congregated to eat and share news, I stopped and hoped for an encouraging word from my friends.

No sooner had I entered the narrow street than a voice lashed at me with a curse. "Ah, here he is, no doubt recently returned from a visit with Michael, that benefactor who asks for proof of craftsmanship." The voice's owner looked at the other men standing with him, and added scornfully, "Here's a fine one, a man who works for free, like every mule, camel and goat."

"Yes," another chimed in. I recognized him, Zacharias, who'd brought me into the trade, teaching me how to hold the tools, shape the wood. "I regret that it is I who taught him." Zacharias shook his head and finger at me. "You fall on troubled times, Luke. But doing business this way hurts all our families. How could you dishonor me this way? Dishonor all those who share your skill, but hold the craft in esteem? You cheapen us all. You've no right to do it. You mustn't do it!"

I opened my palms, unable to defend myself, but wished desperately for words to explain that I loved Ruth, didn't want to lose her. "I haven't taken the job," I managed.

"There is no job," the first man fired back. "There is only work for no money. Everyone suffers right now. And once word of your arrangement with Michael spreads, those few who have shekels to pay will ask for the same terms. You've stolen food from my children's mouths. You are a thief! I'll see you stoned for your crime!" The food market quieted as his frightful words lingered in the air amidst the sweet smells of lamb and roasted peppers.

"*But I haven't taken the job*," I reiterated. "I only went to see what needed to be done." I tried to speak with authority, defiance, but managed to sound only stubbornly childlike, wanting what I want at the expense of those around me.

Zacharias took a few steps forward, protecting me from any immediate harm, and coming close enough to speak that only I might hear.

I wished he had not.

"Luke, your wife is a good woman. But she makes you foolish. It may be her worry over her pregnancy." Zacharias' face softened. "I know you've struggled in this vocation, and I am sorry. But you chose it. You asked for my help, and I gave it. So let me teach you one last thing." His clasped hands pumped twice in emphasis. "There are unspoken rules, loyalties, that men of the wood share. When a tool breaks, another carpenter will gladly lend you his rather than usurp work you cannot finish. When your reputation is at stake for delivering your work on time, another carpenter will assist you without payment. It is our brotherhood, Luke." He smiled with avuncular eyes. "And if you degrade us all by taking this job, you will have forfeited these privileges. Your struggles will increase. Your good wife will wonder what manner of man she has wed, who cannot apply his chosen trade."

My arms fell limp at my sides. I looked Zacharias in the eye, unable to counter anything he'd said. Only one thought came to me. In a voice of abject abandon, I whispered, "But when I did ask for your help, my old friend, at what price did you teach me the beauty of this trade?"

He returned a blank stare.

I answered the question for him. "You taught me for free."

Now utterly alone, I retook my pathway home.

Every reason, every argument for not taking the job streamed through me, most of them uttered from dejected lips under my breath. I believed Zacharias was right, and I feared the threats of the other men. Taking a longer route in returning to my worktables, I considered much. I wanted to reject the entire business and put myself at ease, hoping Ruth could be made to understand. I thought to make my prayers to Yahweh, beseech him for direction. But I could not find the words to supplicate, so filled was I with bitterness for everything, everyone.

In the end, only one piece of wisdom made sense: if I should choose a way, and it led to isolation, poverty, or the unknown, I would choose in keeping with my covenant to Ruth. Zacharias' words injured me. He had often sat at our table, partaking of her supper preparations. That he could speak ill of her made me feel like so much straw stuffed in a sack. Either course seemed to lead to oblivion, but I meant to travel that road with the woman I married.

When I got home, I found Ruth collapsed on the floor. I rushed to her and carried her to the bed, all thoughts of my dilemma pushed aside by a new fear.

"I'm all right," she insisted weakly.

"Nonsense," I argued. "I won't ignore this any longer. You stay in bed, while I go fetch some help."

Ruth protested, but did as I asked as I hurried out into the streets to find someone to tend to her. I quickly came to the residence of a noted midwife and persuaded her to return with me. The stern woman tended Ruth stoically, then gave me simple instructions to keep her well-fed and filled with fluids. Her every word felt like a dagger, an incrimination. In a painful awakening, I realized losing Ruth and the child was a real possibility. *Dear Eternal Father, she faints so often now. Please help us.*

I realized I had to start building the innkeeper's manger as soon as possible. My stock of usable wood had long since been depleted to nothing. The lingering scent of shorn timber remained scarcely a memory. I hadn't enough money to purchase wood, and continued muttering to myself about the opportunity this job had amounted to. Another time, I'd have received an advance for material, and I'd have gone to buy wood from my friend David, who owned the fine olive orchards beyond the city walls. Or, as often happened, my patron would have secured the building supplies himself. None of these options were available to me. Michael the innkeeper had nothing to give. Ruth pretended not to hear my quiet rants, and smiled at me as I considered how to procure the wood.

My first thought was to raise the money for the materials. I had some small items I had made to sell at market. But my attempts there met with little success. Haggling with the streetwise brought me only frustration. Next I followed leads on a few small jobs, hoping to accumulate a large enough sum to build the manger and put some food on the table. But between working in trade and the general hardness of the times, the little jobs only ate away at my time and returned me nothing. All around me others seemed to suffer similar pressures, except those I met hadn't a child coming any week now. I even tried to borrow money, with the promise to repay what I took. But the moneylender I visited turned a deaf ear.

Two days after Ruth collapsed, I realized there was nothing to do but scour the hills and meadows outside the city walls for usable material. Ruth handed me the paltry sum we had left of our savings. "Use this if you don't find what you need," she said, and kissed me goodbye. For the better part of a full day I drew my cart after me in the countryside east of Bethlehem. Hot afternoon sun made the errand unpleasant. Even the shade of the occasional tree provided no respite from the oppressive heat. More than once I started back, having decided to forego this charge and let Ruth think what she wanted of me. Each time, I paused and remembered the vows I took at our wedding, remembered my coming child. Standing beneath the searing sun, the weight of failure bore down on me like the rays of a thousand suns. Still, I could not give up. So long as Ruth held any hope or confidence in me, I had to try again. With that, I walked on, kicking at the ground as I searched for pliable wood. By day's end, I had just enough to create a manger, and headed home to craft and assemble the box.

As I approached home, Ruth ran into the street and embraced me, peeking over my shoulder. When she saw the wood, her arms tightened around my chest. She then promptly placed a plate of cooked vegetables and a cup of water in my hands—her way of saying that she meant for me to work while I ate my supper. I wanted to object, but I held my tongue and took the food as I headed for my tables.

As I set to work, I listened to Ruth hum a melody as she hung our wash to dry. With this prospect, she had found a thread of happiness that she seemed intent on holding until it bore fruit. Every few moments she came to ask me if I needed something more to eat or drink, each offer a transparent excuse to survey my progress.

The elements had cracked and splintered much of the wood. Rough and twisted, it resisted my efforts to remake it into something more than serviceable. "What does it matter," I muttered to myself. "It is a box for beasts to chomp their feed and stuff their bellies. The innkeeper will like whatever I bring him, because I do it for free." In less than an hour I finished, and went in to cool myself with more water.

"Are you finished?" Ruth asked as I poured my cup full again.

"Yes." I took a deep draught of the water and wiped my mouth with my sleeve. "It is finished. Let's just hope your feelings about this man are justified. You really are a fine judge of men," I quipped, trying to make amends.

"May I see it?" Her eyes were bright and expectant.

"Certainly." She rushed to the door and swept out to my tables in the twilight. I filled my cup again before following her. In the violet hues of dusk, I approached. Ruth stood over the manger, unmoving. Coming abreast of her, I saw her face was no longer light and hopeful. She seemed to be considering something altogether grave.

"What is it?" I looked down at the feedbox, unable to see what she seemed to see.

Ruth waited several moments before lifting her soft gaze to meet mine. Her eyes showed concern as she tried to form the words before she spoke. "It is a manger," she said with a rhetorical lilt in her voice.

I nodded, feeling my gut tighten. Slowly, I drew a long breath of cool night air, trying to steady the uneasy feeling growing inside me.

"It will certainly serve," she said with that same unconvinced tone.

"Yes it will," I added with finality.

Clearly she did not approve. Her expression flowed from uneasiness to dismay, then to resolution. Each of them stabbed me, wounding me first, then causing anger to bud in my chest.

"Luke, please understand me. It is a manger, yes, but not the kind of manger you are capable of building. It is not your best work." She paused, coming close to me. I did not turn away, but stared unwaveringly into her upturned eyes. "You must refashion the manger, love. When the man at the inn sees it, there must be no question but that you did your very best work. You mustn't ever do less."

I whirled away from her and called out into the night, as though appealing to a vast court of opinion. "I have spent hours finding wood and making the box, all for nothing! I will receive nothing for it, and our good man at the inn may yet tell me he has no use for my services! I have spent an unbearable day in the scorched hills beyond the city walls. My rest in the shade of cypress trees brought sweat on my brow no less freely than if I'd been running openly in the sun. With no time to sit for supper, I set to work in the dried-over air of sunset, taking poor material into my hands to build something for free. It is absurd! I want to do right by you, Ruth, but you ask too much! This is not the way it is done!"

"You are right," Ruth agreed, her voice quiet in the descending light of day. "This isn't the way it is done. But we need the job, Luke. And I have a feeling the innkeeper needs that manger. Please, work more on it. Do it for me, this one time. I know you are tired. I know the circumstance embarrasses you, but I see it differently. So please, labor on it a while longer." She smiled affectionately, her visage brightening. "Make it the finest manger in Bethlehem!"

I wanted to remain angry. I still felt used and exploited. I still felt like a failure and a poor provider. But looking into the brightness of hope in Ruth's eyes, I could not maintain those feelings. Her smile did not waver, and in that moment my heart spoke to me: Ruth inspired me to be a better man, and if I must always be poor, so be it, as long as I ever held her respect and love. "I will make a great manger," I said and kissed her upon the forehead. I immediately departed for the hills again; it was late, I could not delay.

I needed fresh, pliable wood. I would not find that lying on the ground, but I knew one man who might lend me some. Into the cooling air I went, waving goodbye as I trod up the road. My legs grumbled with aches, but suddenly my commission took hold of me—no longer did I simply work for the innkeeper; now I was building this box for Ruth.

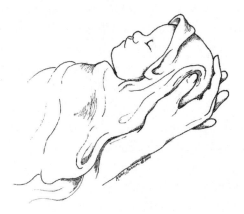

The Handmaiden

The sound of a child's cry is music and ought to bring joy to a mother's heart. That's what I tell them all, each woman whose brow I mop and whose tongue I correct when pained curses fall from their lips during childbirth. I always smile just a little when my words bring that look of bewilderment to their faces. It is the innocence of health and hope that I see there, an innocence that tells me they believe all will be well with their child. I pray they keep these naïve faces until their babes grow old enough to make families of their own. I lost that face long ago.

When I was young I hoped I would not dislike the man I married. In fact, I secretly dreamed I would love him. And when I married an artist, I thought my dream had come true. Our first years together swept by like a summer breeze at dusk, leaving me pleasantly surprised that Eli seemed to know what was important to me without me having to say it.

In the mornings I would wake to find him already up and working. I would step out the back door where he sat and peered toward distant hills to find his inspiration. Hearing me, he always rose and folded me into his arms, whispering, "Good morning," with his warm breath. Then he drew back, an eager look in his eye, and pulled me to sit beside him to view what he'd created.

Some days he worked with paint on vellum, fashioning landscapes so resplendent they rivaled the earth's own beauty. Other days he shared poems with me, words woven together as intricately as a master weaver's most delicate design. These he read to me with a cadence that rose and fell to carry the meaning of the words. Sometimes he nestled my hands between his own and hummed a melody. Eli did not have a pleasant singing voice, but in the early morning light outside our back door, his tunes came to me like the song of birds announcing the dawn.

Eli did not earn much money at his art, but he sold enough at market to buy food and supplies to continue his work. I felt grateful to have found such happiness with him. More grateful still when I found myself with child. One morning I woke before Eli, and took his spot behind our home. When he came out, I stood and hugged him, then made him sit with me and look up the hill.

"We've created something, Eli, something marvelous. Would you like to know what it is?"

He gave me a quizzical look. I took his hand and placed it on my stomach and waited for realization to light in his eyes. When it did,

I knew the blessing of that dear man. Of all the creations he'd been a part of, the pride and joy in our unborn child surpassed them all by leagues.

During the months of my pregnancy, I prepared our home while Eli worked to make the money we would need to support the baby. All day he toiled at different pieces of art to sell at market. But trade in the city ebbed, and he often returned with as much of his art as he took with him. Over his objections, I began small tasks in the homes of women whose husbands prospered in overland trade to other cities, and in the large estates of women whose husbands served in Herod's court. I sewed, washed, and sometimes prepared meals. The work took its toll as my baby grew inside me, but I never shared my exhaustion with Eli because we needed the money.

As it happened, I crossed the street one day to buy some olives from a vendor, and met one of my employers browsing the market with his wife and attendants. I nodded dutifully and quickly turned to go.

Rachel, the lady of the house, called out after me. "Hannah, be still! I've something to say to you." The woman glided past her husband and his servants to take a square stance before me.

I turned, offering a weak smile. "I haven't much time—"

"You will make time!" she interjected. "You left a dirty plate yesterday, and garments that needed washing. I can't suffer sloppy work, Hannah. What excuse have you?"

Her complaint caught me by surprise, and I felt a stab of dread in my heart. Soon after, the heat in the street began to blur my vision. Instinctively, I put a hand over my stomach and reached for a nearby cart to steady myself.

"I see," continued Rachel angrily, "your child makes you lazy and forgetful. Well, perhaps I must seek another handmaid to replace you."

Her voice rose shrilly above the din of the market. Around us, people began to gather, some chuckling behind their hands at the spectacle of me being rebuked openly in public. I swayed, my head suddenly light, and felt a stabbing pain in my navel. I focused on the ground to ease my vision and calm my rapid breath.

"You'll look at me when I address you," Rachel demanded. "I won't be ignored, especially by the wife of a fool."

I looked up then, and my heart went cold as Eli unexpectedly appeared at the edge of the circle of gawkers to see what the trouble was. I tried to straighten, to hide my weakness, and to defend my husband from these insults. But the shooting pain worsened, crackling down my legs. Eli rushed to my side, wrapping an arm around my waist to support me. I realized then, in a way I'd never noticed before, how frail a man my love was. Yet he helped me regain my stance and fixed Rachel with a steely gaze.

"You must be the clown," Rachel spoke sharply to him. "Well, for half a bag of tricks I require half my payment back, Hannah." She gazed at me haughtily. "You woefully neglected the simple jobs of washing and cleaning that any fool could perform. You will return half of what I paid you."

My arms felt heavy, my face hot. I knew my mouth hung open, but I had nothing to say. I tried to blink away the blurred images in my eyes, but nothing could clear them. Sweat ran freely into my eyes. "I cannot," I managed to say. "The money is spent."

"Then you are a thief," Rachel announced to the growing crowd. "An irresponsible woman who gets pregnant by a silly man who cannot support the child, and then steals for him to raise the litter up!"

Anger bloomed behind my eyes, but strength fled my body as the pain in my belly burned and contractions beset me.

I felt Eli's arm tighten protectively around me. "You will not speak to my wife this way. She is greater than you in spirit and character, and will not be returning to your home to pick up after your slovenliness." Eli stood as tall as he could. "Enough of you! Leave us be. What manner of woman takes her thoughts to the open streets, or reviles a woman with child? Say what you will of me, but do not disgrace my wife again."

Rachel's husband, the king's man, emerged from behind her and strode into the center of the circle of spectators. He stood a foot taller than Eli and wore the clothes of a soldier, the emblems of an officer. With a wave of a hand, he motioned for two of his servants to relieve Eli of having to support me. He pointed at my husband and spoke.

"There is a quarrel between our women, but now you have personally insulted me with your insolence toward my wife." He shook a finger. "This will not do. You will defend yourself and your wife's honor—what there is of it." The crowd laughed.

I tried to speak, but my tongue had swelled. I knew that Eli's small, delicate hands and thin shoulders were no match for the soldier. The other man outweighed him by a hundred pounds. I struggled to free myself from the arms of the men that held me, but I was simply too weak.

Eli circled as the soldier pivoted, a chiding smirk on his face. Then in a flurry, the larger man slammed his fists several times into

Eli's face and chest, pounding him to the ground. Eli gave all he could to his defense, to stand for my honor. But his hands were not made to fight. He was an artist. In the streets of Bethlehem, he fell bloodied to the ground.

The other man kicked him relentlessly. I cried out, but the cheers and shouts of the onlookers overwhelmed my feeble protests. Eli attempted to cover himself and roll away. Each time the man caught him and the beating continued. A chorus rose around the soldier who brutalized my husband. The guards who held me loosened their grips, distracted by the fight. Ripping my hands free, I broke away and rushed to Eli's defense. The guards pursued me. And as I placed myself between Rachel's husband and Eli, one of the guards shoved me harshly to the ground and kicked me in the ribs. A roar of disapproval rose from the crowd. With the shift in sentiment, the fight was over. Weak and unskilled in the art of combat, Eli lay crushed and broken.

The three assailants backed away cautiously, merging into the crowd. Rachel sniffed before turning and following her husband up the street. Slowly, the crowd departed, save a few men who carried Eli home, and an elderly woman who helped me stagger into my bed.

My baby was coming. I felt too weak to deliver the child, and beside myself with worry for Eli. But the baby was coming all the same. My skin slick with sweat, I felt alternately hot and cold. The fever in my face and cheeks spread down my neck, wrapping my entire body like a wave of flame. Somewhere in my delirium, I called for Eli. Shortly after, a man entered the room with a grave face. He shared a look with the old woman who sat over me. As she turned back to me, I knew Eli was dead.

All the sounds of my grief caught deep in my throat behind a simple, profound sob that stole my breath. My soul felt as though it had been divided, part of me torn away. A meek, loving man had stood beside me to declare my worth, and he now lay dead in the outer room. The will to give birth to my child fled me.

The old woman studied my face, then huddled close. "Listen to me," she said in an urgent but caring voice. "Whatever else may be true, you are this babe's mother. It depends on you, and you mustn't forsake it before its life is even begun." She leveled a determined eye. "I won't have it. We share a sisterhood, you see." She leaned closer still. "It is a special call, dear, and from the Most High. Put your pain aside, my child. You are weak, but do not falter. Your husband did what he had to do. And so now must you. I will be here, and I won't leave you until we've seen it through."

I looked into her face, this gentle woman who had struggled to carry me to my bed. Her skin appeared like wrinkled parchment; from her hairline and neck, large brown spots crept forward onto her brow and cheeks. She had a hawkish nose, over which her eyes burned bright and sure.

I nodded.

Throughout the night I labored to bring my child into the world with the help of that good woman—a stranger less than a day ago. She dampened my forehead with a cold, wet cloth. She spoke words of encouragement, added oil to the lamp, and incanted the most glorious prayers as she went about her ministrations. I heard the removal of my beloved Eli's body in the dark hours of night . . . leaving me alone with this woman, this stranger, to begin a new life with my baby and no husband.

And, still, I labored. Each time I faltered, I replayed the horrible scene from the street over in my head, using my anger at the unfairness of it, to coax my body into the necessary work of giving birth.

Then my child began to come. I could feel the moment drawing nigh, and the old woman sat urging the infant from my womb. At last, I pushed a final time and felt immense relief flood every muscle in my body. I lay limp in my bed, a small ray of hope shining inside me at the thought of sharing with this new life the wonderful creations Eli had already made to entertain the child. I imagined sitting in our spot—Eli's and mine—with my baby, recounting the moments I had spent there in the glory of dawn with the child's father.

The candle guttered. I raised my head enough to see the old woman and ask the sex of my babe. The image of her countenance haunts me still: ashen, drawn, closer to the grave. She looked up at me. Without seeing the newborn, I knew it had arrived as cold as Eli.

Too weak to cry, I collapsed back into my bed and could do no more than feel the woolen sheets wet with the sweat of my labor itching my skin. What sisterhood is there in this? I thought bitterly. What dear, honored thing is the birth of a still child?

The old woman stayed with me for weeks, nursing me back to health. She never spoke of the night we met, or of Eli, or of her stern words that compelled me to deliver my baby. She only fed me, washed me, sang as she moved about the house, filling it with sound, with life.

Eventually, I rose from my bed. With the desire no more to clean up after others, I learned from the old woman the delicate skills of a midwife, handmaid to childbirth. By the time the old woman followed Eli and my child to the grave a year later, I knew all I needed to support myself alone.

I became familiar with the quiet hours of evening. I sat up often, remembering vividly the events of that one, horrible night. In the silence that settled over Bethlehem when the day was well gone, I often thought I heard sounds echoing forward in time. Sounds that marked off the hours up to the moment when I had purged my body. Those solitary nights drew out like a blade, growing taut and uncomfortable, sharp and dangerous. Safe as I was, I nevertheless always felt a breath away from my own final resting place in the earth.

The years marched by. Countless children did I usher into the world. Children like the daughter born to the king's sister, Heziah.

Her home stood on the north side of the palace. Long, high walls hung with the richest tapestries, and the wood glistened with a fresh rub of olive oil. Fragrant incense sweetened the air, which shifted with cool breezes that crossed the light rooms and halls through high windows.

Several servants and attendants bustled within, and conducted me to her room. Propped up on her bed with silk pillows, she directed her day of childbirth as she no doubt directed everything else. And people jumped at her command. Deep in my memory, I saw the face of Rachel who had shamed me in the street the day Eli died. Heziah shared the same tone of voice. I shook the memory away and proceeded to her bed.

"You sent for me," I said simply, coming abreast of her.

The lady looked up, having to look twice before realizing that I was not one of her regular handmaids. A familiar expression touched her features, one I've grown accustomed to: the look of an expectant mother who stares up into a face slack and pale, and filled with none of the excitement she feels herself. Better for them because I've seen the panic of such an event paralyze a less stony handmaid.

"Yes," she finally said. Turning to the others she commanded, "Leave us." A contingent of guards and servants stepped from the room, leaving only a young girl who stood opposite me awaiting an order. "Bring some water," Heziah said. The girl went to her task.

"Your position is good," I commented, pulling my sleeves back. With the water the girl brought I washed and came to stand at the foot of the woman's bed. "You are particularly calm," I observed.

As she started to answer, her face twisted in pain. Labor began in earnest. The usually decorous woman spat vile things from her mouth. She clawed at the expensive sheets on her bed. A strange kind of hatred burned in her eyes when she looked at me from between her knees. I suppressed the smile that often comes to me in such moments, because I knew the hatred was not for me, but blind anger born of pain and urgency.

The tall ceilings resounded with her cries and grunts. I set my hands to their work as stolidly as the old woman had done for me years ago. Perhaps that was why I followed the old woman into such a vocation: women all traveled to the same valley when they birth their children, and I, possessing a steadiness that other women lack, had chosen to remain in that valley.

With no complications, Heziah's child arrived. A baby girl as perfect and healthy as could be hoped. Fresh, pinkish skin glistened in the light of the room, and momentarily the babe took a lungful of air and let out a cry that resounded as loudly as her mother's colorful speech.

I wiped the child clean and prepared her in a new wrap. Then to Heziah I presented this newest soul to her mother. As I handed over the girl, whimpers and mutters ascended from the infant's lips. The same pain touched my heart that entered each time I assisted a life into this world. Long ago I had held promise closely to my breast: a husband who loved me, a child inside me. That life had been ripped away. The clean, gentle smell of a baby reminded me of the lifeless body of my own stillborn child. But there, in the lap of opulence, health abounded, the blessing of life to one that knows only luxury, who can afford an army of servants and a handmaid besides.

"Your child lives," I said, as I always did, the meaning of it clear only to me. "Her cry is music to a mother's heart."

I watched the mother hold her child a moment before she called her attendant over and handed the infant to her. Strength seemed to return to the feisty woman quickly, and a hoarse bark brought others rushing into the room to do her bidding. The child was borne away to some other place, no doubt to a wet nurse.

I gathered my belongings and received a small payment on my way out. I stopped to take a last look at the stained sheets on the bed, and to think about the perfect health of the woman's child. I watched her wave a dismissive hand toward me, and quietly I retook myself to the streets and home.

When I arrived, a young man stood waiting at my door. His tunic hung loose around his shoulders and waist, and his face bore the look of infrequent meals. He hastily introduced himself as Luke.

"Please," he said, before I'd even reached the door, "my wife, Ruth, is long with child, but she has begun to faint often. Just now she collapsed. I fear for her health and the life of the babe."

Sighing, I pushed him aside with my bag. "Give me a moment." I went inside and washed my face and drank a cup of water. After changing my apron, I joined the man on my step, and together we departed.

Luke's modest home was clean, though the usual scents of warming food were noticeably absent. Still, when I sat on the edge of his wife's bed, she greeted me with a cheerful smile.

I touched the back of my hand to her cheek. "You're pale," I observed. "Have you been eating well?"

Ruth looked over my shoulder at her husband and offered, "I haven't had the energy to keep up with the housework—"

"Dear one," I interrupted, "that was not my question." I saw her unease at my directness—the young haven't the stomach to be plain. "You keep an ordered home," I offered, softening my candor. "But if I'm to be of any help to you, I must have straight, honest answers."

Sharing another look with her husband behind me, Ruth admitted, "We've had no work for several weeks. And our surviving family live far from us. We have little food . . . and what there is, we ration." Then she added with a hopeful smile, "My husband is a carpenter and must have strength to work. He will have a job soon at the inn."

I turned to gather the truthfulness of the statement from the look in Luke's eyes. The emptiness there did not reassure me.

I looked back at the frail woman sweating on her bed. I soaked a rag in a bowl of water and dabbed her lips. They would not have money to pay me. In truth, there may never be a need; she might lose the child before it had a chance for life. The thought brought my own birthing-bed back to me like a shard of wood beneath a fingernail. Though a different kind of artist, this carpenter was not so different from my Eli. Before I could name any further similarities, the woman asked, "Will you help us when the time comes?"

When I began this life of a handmaiden, a midwife, a friend to women in their most needful hour, I had done so because of the kindness shown me by another. "Don't concern yourself with such things," I answered. "Rest. And eat larger portions than you are eating now. This child inside you depends on you for its sustenance." I placed the rag back in the bowl and stood to go.

The carpenter followed me from the room, escorting me to the door. He wore his embarrassment openly. "I *am* trying to find work," he said, his tone apologetic, betraying deeper fears that must have scourged him incessantly.

I meant to say something to allay his worries, but my own shard of memory stung me still.

"Watch her close," I advised. "Give her more to eat, more to drink, however hard it may be for you to do it. Come for me when you must."

He nodded solemnly. And I left.

I sat in my darkened house that night and pondered injustice. Twice that day had I stared it in the face. Seated before my hearth, I stared again, this time into the fire, finding some comfort in the blaze. Looking up, I saw the pieces of art Eli had created for our baby, our son, at least in body. I realized how many creations there were, and with abrupt fury they mocked me, each one cried as a voice from the grave. In a bitter rush I gathered all the art—each parchment, everything—and cast it all into the fire. The flames licked and flared at the dry tinder. In a moment, those treasures were gone, never to be reclaimed from the ashes . . . Sadness welled within me, but I refused to let it touch my face. Quelling the memories and loneliness, I went to bed.

On night a few days later, a quiet rap came at my door. Long into the evening hours already, it could only be a call to assist a mother in giving birth. Before going to the door, I gathered my things and wrapped my black shawl around my shoulders.

Through the streets I followed a man who continually checked over his shoulder to be sure he hadn't lost me. But I did not run. My haste would not get me there in time to do anything more than walking would. Nor did it feel like a night to rush. A strange, expectant feeling resided in the streets of Bethlehem, far different from the tone of my home in these same late hours.

The man led me toward a familiar inn. More than one child had I helped into life there. He surprised me by passing the inn, hurrying instead toward a small stable burrowed into the hill. These kinds of quarters kept livestock safer, but I hoped there was not a mistake— I did not work with animals.

Into the stable I followed the man, who retired behind a young woman who lay atop a blanket spread on a bed of straw. I wondered if it itched the way my bed of wool had the night I gave birth. The woman's husband knelt beside her, their hands fastened together. A cursory glance told me they had no money. Their clothes were stained and dirty; the man's feet worn as from travel. It was likely they had come into Bethlehem to be counted and taxed. Weariness rested on their features, but so too did a mildness, a kindness unlike the parents of most the children I'd cupped in my hands.

"We've little to offer you," the man said, as if determining my hesitation.

His eyes settled on me with a tenderness, the way Eli's eyes used to. Slightly larger of frame, the expectant father nevertheless appeared like a creative man, one who might also fashion things with his hands. His meekness very likely cost he and his wife much, but no doubt remained one of the very things she loved about him.

The woman offered me a smile, the same hope and health in her face I'd noted a hundred times before. Yet somehow it seemed different this time. Perhaps because this fair, young girl looked poor and tired the way I had been when my hour of delivery came. Perhaps because she lay on a bed of straw in a stable dug from a hill behind a traveler's inn. I let down my black shawl and called for water.

Never leaving her side, the man, whom his wife addressed as Joseph, watched me silently, a kind of trust in the set of his lips and brow that I had not seen before. But the woman, whom he lovingly called Mary, had come to the same valley that we all do when giving birth, giving life. Despite her obvious courage, trepidation crossed her fair face. Some women let their fright and pain out with foul language. Mary did not, even though genuine concern showed each time I asked something of her.

"Will it be all right?" she asked Joseph, imploring him for reassurance.

He caught my eye, seeming to measure me. Never dropping my gaze, he answered, "We are in good hands. Yahweh has seen to it."

Mary did not appear completely convinced. I don't blame her. Men can't know all that a woman feels in those moments of deepest agony and hope. So I inclined close and favored her bright, fair eyes with a stern but loving look. My old life danced across my memory. I heard a quavering voice speaking in my mind. Listening close, I spoke the words to Mary. "Listen to me," I said. "Whatever else may be true, you are this babe's mother. It depends on you and you mustn't forsake it before its life is even begun." I leveled a determined eye on the young girl. "I won't have it. We share a sisterhood, you see." I leaned closer still. "It is a special call, dear, and from the Most High. Put your pain aside, my child. You are weak, but do not falter." Thinking of Joseph's dirty feet, I went on. "Your husband did what he had to do. And so now must you. I will be here, and I won't leave you until we've seen it through."

Great tears of gratitude welled in young Mary's eyes, and she nodded. Over the next few hours I spoke softly to her, instructing her in what to do. Joseph did not speak or move, but held his wife's hand and helped bear her pain. The night waxed on, and a few others gathered in the front of the stable. I put them right out to keep this moment private. They didn't argue with me, fortunately for them.

When the moment arrived, I smiled at the expectant mother and said a silent prayer. I wanted that lovely young woman who'd shown real gratitude and confidence in my help to have a healthy child. Softness touched the air, mildness even in that gamy stable. And we three together shared a breath of joyful relief when at last the babe came forth into the world. I took the small infant cupped in my hands and watched his delicate features as he drew his first mortal breath. With it came a splendid cry that he lived, and might know the joys of life and love. My heart swelled, grief receded, and all the promise of life that Eli had blessed me with, rushed in again. I noted with sweet irony that the death of my own son had set me on the path that led me to the manger to help deliver the child-king. Looking at the babe, beauty filled my eyes as surely as it had the morning I first told my husband of our own son.

I held the boy and knew suddenly the joy of motherhood, believed somehow that I would meet my son again someday. That there did exist a beautiful place, as lovely as Eli's painting, where my child and I would walk on the grass and listen to Eli's funny morning songs.

I smiled at Joseph, and found the same sure look that had rested on his strong features moments before, as though his faith in me had never wavered. But more, as though his faith in my being there was as sure as the straw beneath his feet. Suddenly, the night no more held me captive, nor did the past.

Placing the babe in Mary's arms, I announced, "Your child lives." I paused, feeling warmth running down my own cheeks. With a quavering voice I continued, "His cry is music to a mother's heart . . . yours and mine."

Twice a Gift

Never spending too long in one place, I've traveled through Judaea, Samaria, Galilee, and up and down the ports of the Great Sea, and sometimes was nearly caught by the king's men or Caesar's guards. The king's men were easy to elude, but because of Hebrew laws about graven images, Caesar's men masked their legionary standards in deference to the Sanhedrin, making them more difficult to spot. Ultimately, it didn't matter. The night always cloaked my escape, and I was blessed with hasty feet.

Long ago I abandoned the name of my birth. To most I was called Boots, because I did not wear sandals, but full footwear fashioned from the hide of a bull. I laced them high, and usually wrapped them with dirty rags to hide their strangeness to sandal wearers. But I would not have traded them for anything. My boots conveyed me swiftly whenever flight was necessary. Or else they hid my passage, soft and quiet, as I treaded upon the rooftops or back-streets of unsuspecting homes. My skill was to reap what others sowed, and it didn't pay to tarry in one spot.

That was how I came to Bethlehem.

On the high roads that connect various towns and villages, I spent many hours considering the morality of my profession. There was always one argument that couldn't be disproved: I was not qualified to do anything else. Religious men would have exhorted me to repent and offer my body to the physical labors of the working class. But those were often the same men who would sit in their royal robes and collect tithes from the poor, on which they sup while reclining in the heated hours of midday. No, I reasoned, I had one very decided skill, and I used it to my best advantage. As I moralized on the high roads, the last word on the topic was this: that life was a difficult trail, and the only standard of measure, it seemed, was to make it through alive. Every man must do what he can to live one day to the next, and I found my way to meet that standard—I met the test. Others could judge if they chose, but it wouldn't protect their goods if I knew they had bounty to spare.

I generally made it a point not to thieve from the poor. Usually, they hadn't much worth taking, but what they did have they deserved to keep. At times, I wondered if things might have been different for me had my parents had provided more than the paltry shack and mule I grew up with, but I tried not to philosophize about it too much. It was enough to say that the poor had nothing to fear from me.

So I studied the wealthy. A man with money was easy to identify. The wealthy have an easy gait. They are often reserved, rarely in a hurry, and have the narrow glare of greed even as they stroll the market. A modest man, even if well dressed, sweats too liberally at the prospect of spending some of what he has. Yet, he too has money. And after in a mere hour upon the streets I generally had a week's work of 'wages' ahead of me.

The trick to surviving as a thief in the land of Judaea, was for the thief to be modest in his takings. A smart burglar would gain rapid entrance, spy no more than two small, preferably light, valuables and take his leave before he could breathe a dozen times. The man seated next to him at the tavern from which he departed on his underhanded business would always vouch for his whereabouts because the thief was never gone long enough for him to notice, so long as he returned promptly. And I knew that if I took reasonable items, the wealthy were likely to go weeks before noticing their absence. By then, I'd be moralizing again upon the high roads, and resting by a small fire with meat in my stomach and wine in my skins.

Bethlehem was no different. At least, not at first.

The day I arrived, I cultivated shallow friendships in one of the local taverns. To do this, I dressed the part; in the working sections of the cities I visited, it was wise not to appear too prosperous. Blending in was not too difficult—faces in the poor areas tended to blur together because of the sheer number of them, and so a stranger might be a permanent resident as far as his drinking mate was aware.

Other than my boots, I looked like every man who had ever come to, lived in, or died at Bethlehem. None of this was arbitrary.

My second day in Bethlehem I attended the market. The smell of spices and animals mingled in the warming air. Chatter erupted in bursts from carts and stands as food and goods were bartered, traded, and bought. The sky was an unrivaled blue without any thr}at of clouds. I walked with my eyes cast toward the ground to conceal the defining features of my face. Toward the wealthy end of the market I walked, where watchful merchants neatly displayed fine cloths, writing instruments, and undamaged foods. In Bethlehem, this area of the market was aligned in the shadows of high walls, keeping it cool and pleasant for those who could afford to shop for the more expensive wares.

I sat on the ground near a doorway and pulled my wrap about my nose and mouth, to watch closely as the rich came to parade, swagger and make witty comments, and be seen by one another. Of course, the wealthiest men never came, for they had servants to perform those errands for them. It was never wise to attempt to steal from *those* homes. They were likely to have a small squad of the city guard assigned to them, and the men that owned such homes were the type to make a daily accounting of all they possessed. Instead, I looked for those who were careless enough to make a show of their social standing. In an hour I had spied my first target.

A tailor displayed some high-quality tunics, robes, and veils. He bore the infirmity of a severe stoop in his posture, and seated himself to make watching his wares easier. Over the course of several hours he turned a brisk business. Some of his clients had the potential to be targets, but I could never pull myself away from the idea that this diminutive tailor had a stash of money which he hoarded for himself. His clothes did not reflect a life of wealth—a curious wrap of cloth around his chest, like bandages or swaddling—but the severity in the miser's eyes led me to choose him as my first job.

I discreetly followed him home, noting the place of his residence. Then, as was my practice, I left the city. Once far enough away that I was completely alone, I ran—sprinting, stopping, jumping, and sprinting again. I had learned long ago that stealth had everything to do with agility and speed, and that was my routine to keep my feet and legs nimble and strong. If a situation grew threatening, I had to know that my feet and boots could bear me away safely. When my body grew tired, I stopped beneath a tree and slept until dusk. Then, by the light of a westering sun, I reentered Bethlehem and went straight to the tavern.

I kept a kind of quiet company with several of the other men, speaking only infrequently. I drank a few cups of wine, nodding with disinterest at their commentary about the demise of King Herod and the ineptness of his son, Archelaus. For hours I listened to them prattle about their wives, their plans for wealth, and whatever else drifted from their inebriated brains. Only one man noticed my strange footwear, so I gave him a wide berth for the remainder of the evening—observant men are the bane of any man who lives by stealth.

When it seemed least conspicuous, I took my leave and crept to the home of the tailor. With little trouble I gained entrance through a window, and searched specifically for the implements of his trade. Average-minded men and women believe nothing is so inconspicuous as the ordinary items they use every day. For precisely this reason they are given to hiding their valuables in or near these things.

Finding his sewing box, I emptied it and found a hollow compartment in the base. A full bag of silver, with some gold coins mixed in, was my prize.

In less time than it took to drawn thirty breaths, I had my booty and was out the window. No one had missed me when I retook my seat at the inn's tavern and common room.

The next day I visited the market again to choose a second target.

The man was tall and well fed. His clothes were garish like the feathers of a peacock, his beard clean and trimmed. He stood at the table of a merchant who sold perfumed veils. One by one the peacock picked them up with a flourish and put them to his majestic nose.

"A very nice choice, sir. Our finest handiwork, Egyptian linen, and quite reasonable." The merchant spoke in musical tones, his words like a singsong of friendship and betrayal.

"It smells too much like olives. I want one that is like the bloom of water-flowers." He tossed the veil back to the table.

The merchant quickly replaced the veil with another. This one was a deep russet color. The tall customer took it and brought it to his great nose.

His eyes widened, then closed as he breathed deeply. "Ah, this is what I want. She will intoxicate me with this fragrant scent." His eyes shifted, affecting disinterest. "How much?"

The two men haggled for a few moments before money was exchanged and the tall man walked on with a self-satisfied smile.

Next he came to a pitiful booth displaying a number of delicate woodwork pieces fashioned with exquisite care. The time spent attending to small details, rendering intricacies in the faces of figurines, the fur of animals, the leaves on a tree, showed the expert abilities of the craftsman.

The tall, well-fed man perused the items with indifference, until, one item caught his attention—an elegant castle built of wood shavings, with thin, fluted pillars, parapets, and wooden flags unfurled and flying in imagined winds. The whole piece rested in the palms of his hands. He smiled over it, betraying his interest to buy.

Clearing his throat, he asked the merchant its price. "It's so small. It can't have taken long to make," he reasoned. "What do you want for it?"

A thin man stood from behind the makeshift table, his frame looking haggard in the glare of the sun. His apparent desperation to sell made him overly eager, and he stumbled over his words. "This is the best piece, the best in the market. I can sell it cheap. Make me an offer."

At that, the man handled the item casually, unappreciatively. He looked from the merchant to the wooden castle and back. "I know you, do I not?"

The man smiled sheepishly. "I built the fence behind your home. I am a carpenter by trade. My name is—"

"I thought as much," the well-fed man interjected. "A shoddy piece of work. I should wonder if this trinket is equally inferior."

"I assure you," the carpenter argued, "that this is quality work. The skill necessary to create the pillars, the flags—"

In his diffidence, the tall, well-fed man dropped the castle to the street, where all the delicate intricacies broke or snapped. The carpenter rushed around his table and knelt to the destroyed piece. The well-fed man sniffed haughtily. "I told you it was not well made.

Get it off the street before I have the authorities remove you for a swindler." With that, he walked off.

I was decided. He would be my second mark.

Cautiously, I trailed him to his home. There was an entrance from the alley on the side of his house, and several windows. With so many hidden ways to enter, his would be an easy home to rob. Slowly, I disappeared back into the swirl of humanity.

Then, I went once more into the hills to run and stretch my legs. Afterward, I returned to the tavern as before.

I waited two nights before moving on the well-fed man. Suspicion would be high after the first job. It was wise to wait a time before striking again. I strolled the market in the days between, but not to choose a third mark. It was prudent for me to mingle in the tight crowds, so the people might say, "I've seen him before," without being able to place the time or moment. Not being a stranger would lend credibility to my defense if ever I were caught.

I likewise exercised my body, spending a few hours each day on the roads beyond the city, running, sprinting, all the usual routines. After night had fallen fully on the second day, I left my chair in the common room tavern and quietly slipped out into the darkness. I stole to the home of the tall, well-fed man and found no light within. Calmly, I drew close to the wall beneath a window and checked the alley for passersby. There were none. In one lithe movement I turned, jumped, and took hold of the sill. I pulled myself to the window, swung my legs over and crouched just inside. My landing sounded like nothing so much as a garment being placed upon the floor.

Usually, I would have waited for my eyes to adjust to the deeper darkness of the home's interior. But the light from the night sky was bright, lighting the room with a pale glow. Without moving, I took inventory of the room. The size of the bed and the fine decorating convinced me that I'd entered the bedroom of the master of the house.

Placing my feet gingerly, I crept about the room, inspecting every recess. In the space of sixteen breaths I found the item I wanted. Spying a golden box, most likely used for holding jewelry and whatever coins the man carried with him, I flexed my fingers and lifted the item. Carefully, I drew back the lid. Angling the small container toward the light from the window, within I found a necklace fashioned of silver, strung with a beautiful stone pendant. It was a great find, but surely something that would be quickly missed. Even so, the price of such a piece of jewelry would be high on the open road, and I could afford to leave Bethlehem with this one night of work.

In four more breaths I was out in the alley again, the necklace tucked deeply within my tunic. I walked casually, as though tired from a day of work, and went directly back to my chair in the tavern. I debated staying the night at the inn. I could leave by dawn's light and be safely away from Bethlehem before any investigation could be conducted.

Retaking my chair, I ordered a cup of wine, and nodded to the man on my right as though I hadn't missed a moment of his rambling. That night I felt that I was doubly blessed. Fortune had handed me an expensive necklace, and the inn resounded with games and laughter as men played at being Caesar by answering the questions of the patrons. I asked no question of my own, but laughed with the rest, occasionally patting my breast to feel the jut of the necklace. I raised my drink to toast my luck, knowing that no one missed me, and that a jovial crowd would be the strongest alibi should an inquiry come.

As the evening waned, a man entered the tavern and took a seat beside me.

To no one in particular he said in an abject voice, "I wish I had something to give them."

Usually, it was my practice to make a quiet, indecipherable sound of agreement. Enough to acknowledge, but not enough to encourage, conversation. But this time, I was intrigued and wanted to know what the man meant. It would violate my own code—direct words invited eye contact, the opportunity for another to study my features and easily identify me later. But the feeling would not cease, perhaps because my experience did not offer me many examples of charity. I'd seen the man begging drinks all night. What could inspire a leech such as this to charity?

"To whom do you wish to give?" I asked, keeping my eyes directed cautiously forward.

The man swiveled in his seat, scrutinizing me closely. I did not return his gaze, but sat calmly, waiting for him to explain. Then, his rough hand settled over mine. The gesture disarmed me. Not a sentry with chains to bind, and not a merchant with lucre to purchase stolen goods. This man touched me with a sincerity that robbed me of my mistrust.

He swallowed, preparing to speak. "A woman has given birth to a child in the stables behind the inn. She and her husband's clothes are soiled from the dirt of the high roads. They rest with the animals because the inn was full, and the lady had need of a place to give birth to her babe."

I forgot my suspicion and turned round to him. "Surely room could have been made. No child ought to take its first breath from the fragrance of a stable."

The man smiled and patted my hand. "Youth," he said, "such a sense of equanimity they have. It is worth holding, my young friend. But a grasp upon it becomes difficult with age." He squeezed my fingers. "Still, this birth is special. This child . . ." He trailed off, taking a close look at my face.

On another day, I might have felt uncomfortable, might have excused myself. In the common room of the inn, one hand holding my wine, the other warm beneath the old fellow's wrinkled hand, I could only think of a child born so low that this poor man wanted to offer a gift and could not.

Then a look of understanding spread across the wizened face. At once, I believed he had discovered my illicit occupation, but also had found a kind of redemption from his own dilemma by the knowledge.

The old man hooked his second hand behind my neck and pulled me close. Pocked skin hung beneath his eyes like drapes from windows. So near him, I saw strands of black and grey hair intertwining as they twisted from his pores. He wetted his lips with a thick tongue, and smiled broadly, showing me well-used teeth. And still, such happiness I can't remember ever seeing.

"You're my gift, my young friend," he whispered. "By sharing the news with you, I'll have passed along the most valuable thing I own."

He waited, as though some epiphany might dawn in my face at any moment.

I stared, unenlightened.

"Do an old man a favor, young man," he said, insistence clear in his voice. "Take yourself out to the stables. Put aside your own private labors, your opinions about me, and your wine. Go see the child in the manger." His eyes never wavered.

I drew my last gulp of wine with a sour tongue. Less because the wine was bad, and more because yet another child had come into this life destined to poverty and tribulation. Born in a stable! I looked at my boots and hoped the child would not need to wear such a pair. Perhaps he would have a keen, swift mind and have no need to pass as *quietly* through this world as I.

Without thinking further upon it, I untangled myself from the old man and stepped into the night. Welcome darkness enfolded me, an old friend to be sure. But whether affected by the urgency of the man's words, or something else entirely, the night touched my skin as an invitation I could not name. Not as thief, not as law-breaker. Confused, I strode to the stable, where a small gathering of well-wishers stood reverently beneath the light of a brilliant star. Walking toward them, I realized the star had been the source of my light in the bedroom of the tall, well-fed man.

I took a place near the front and looked in at the parents. The husband sat behind his wife, his arms cradling her as she gazed on her son. Some of those who had come had placed gifts at the foot of the manger the child used for a bed. None of these things would do much to help him; they had no real value to buy food or provide shelter.

Would the parents provide for the child? How close were they to taking residence with the row of beggars at the city wall? I found my heart pounding in my chest at the thought of a young boy forced to steal to fill his belly. I cringed at the thought of a mother or father seated at a bare supper table, trying to answer a boy's hunger . . . and unable to do it. I thought of a boy running on an open road, running with all the strength in his possession, to leave behind the ache of guilt, of hunger. The ache of failure that could crush strong men, batter hopeful women, and tear at the bonds of family.

Cautiously, I produced the necklace from the folds of my tunic. For a second time, I looked at my boots. How might the child look were he to wear them?

The light of the large star gleamed dimly off the cut of the stone as I contemplated making a gift of it to the babe. Then a heavy hand rested on my shoulder. I nearly took flight in a move of self-preservation, knowing surely that the hand belonged to a local authority.

Trying to remain calm, I looked at the owner of the hand and nearly dropped the necklace: it was the tall, well-fed man from whom I had taken the jewelry.

He smiled at me and looked at the treasure in my fingers. He did not speak. Nor did I. But we shared a look in that peaceful stillness near the bed of a newborn child who had come into the world as poor and hopeless as I.

Finally, I extended the necklace to the large man, hoping he would accept it as a peace offering. He smiled gently. "No, my friend," he intoned quietly, "you keep it. I have no need of it anymore." He squeezed my shoulder affectionately and resumed his vigil upon the infant as quickly as that. Faster than I had ever stolen anything in my life, he'd forgiven my crime. I marveled. *Was this the same man who had callously discarded the craftsman's tiny castle that day in the market? What was it about this night that had warmed a heart as cold as his?*

My fingers felt numb, and I'm certain my jaw hung low from disbelief. How would I moralize now on the high roads as I passed from city to city? I fingered the pendant in my hands, caressing its molded smoothness and intricate edges. As I looked down at it, I could not help but see, again, my boots.

Without thinking, I stepped through the crowd and approached the feed-box as quietly as ever I did anything in my special footwear. I bent and placed the necklace near the other gifts. I turned to rejoin the crowd when something occurred to me, something I needed to say. I bent and retook the piece of jewelry in my benumbed fingers. I thumbed it over in my palm, before slowly holding it out to the fair woman beside the manger.

"Please, dear lady, use this that the boy might never have to walk among men and cloak his steps."

The woman gently took the necklace and embraced me.

I haven't any reason for explaining why I began to weep on her shoulder, but she held me and whispered into my ear. "Dear friend, at the far end of Bethlehem, just beyond the gate, sits an old woman begging alms. Her clothes are dirty and her back is bent low from so many difficult years. I had nothing to give her when I came, but I so wanted to offer her something."

She drew back to look into my eyes. "How quickly could you take this necklace to her?"

I cried, the salty tears dropping onto my lips. "Fair woman, I will run as fast as ever I have and take it to her."

She kissed my cheek and whispered, "Run."

I stood and stepped past the crowd and took to my heels. Never did I run faster than that night. With the light of the star and the feel of my boots, I might have been flying as I raced through Bethlehem.

A Night of Peace

I sat on the edge of the strange bed, rocking back and forth. *What had I done*? Behind me slept a large man, a stranger. He snored loudly, his body strong with the musk of hard work. I stared across the room at the table beside the door, a handful of coins loosely piled there. The very sight of them soured my stomach; and I closed my eyes to calm the churning inside. *Was this how Mother provided for me*? My mind raced, a torrent of images cascading down upon me, each more painful than the last.

Thankfully, anger pushed the pain aside. Mother had spoken ill of Father because he had been a gambler, one of those who travel by camel and donkey with a host of other dubious fellows. He worked one town until the people pushed him out, tired of his schemes and laughter late into the night.

I saw only him once: a fat man with a belly laugh, and lots of tin rings upon his fingers. He didn't recognize, but I suppose that was all right. I only knew *him* because my mother pointed him out before leading me quickly away and admonishing me: "Rebekah, you must never seek him out. Do you understand? He is no good for you."

But how better was her life as a woman of the street, a woman of flesh and shadows? Staring at the coins awaiting me across the room, I wished detestable things on her for that moment. Little did I know that the heavy breathing of the man behind me would become familiar to me because the choices in my life had been few. No true friends does a harlot have. And fewer still, her quiet daughter.

Chills ran up my back. Not because of the cold, but because of the closeness to the grave I suddenly felt. I stood up from the soiled bed and crept to the fire to warm myself, huddling to rub my hands in the glow. The man turned over. I froze, hoping he would not wake. I had nothing to say, and I wanted to think of someplace to go—I could not imagine going home again.

Gradually, I understood the fullness of what I had just done. I felt the weight of all the night press down upon me. I expected the roof to cave in, darkness to descend, and smother me. I only hoped it would not be as cold as what I was feeling. Somehow I could not get warm enough.

Hunkering close to the embers, I drew a half-burnt stick from the fire. I held up the smoking end, turning it, examining it, breathing in the smell of spent ash. The stick quickly cooled, and I randomly pulled it across the floor around my toes, tracing my feet with the darkened tip. Scooting back, I saw the shape of my feet, and took the smallest delight in my drawing.

Then, suddenly, an image blossomed unbidden in my head. Something so strong, so forceful, that the uneasiness and filth of this first night receded before it.

Grasping the thought, I stood and searched the room for some parchment. I felt stiffness in my legs and hips that I would one day grow accustomed to, but just then I was too intent on having something to draw upon. I spied an unrolled scroll in a shallow basket, and tiptoed to retrieve it. Carefully, I removed it and quickly retook my place before the fire. Immediately, I committed to papyrus the image in my head. I worked fast, my hands suited to the movements, creating with precision the form in my mind. The scratching of the stick over the parchment lulled my senses; I lost myself in the art. When the charred end became no longer useful, I placed it in the coals to char it again. Once withdrawn from the fire, I waited impatiently for the stick to stop smoking before beginning afresh. With smoke lingering about my head, I set again to my drawing. Somewhere along the way, warmth replaced the bitter cold in my bones.

"What's going on here!" boomed a voice from behind me. I dropped the stick, whipping around as the man got up from the bed. "I don't pay money for you to play with the fire! Why don't you make yourself useful and cook something to eat?"

I stammered something incoherent and retreated to the corner.

The man took three threatening steps toward me, his large body blocking the light of the lamp upon the table. Sitting in his shadow,

I pulled my drawing to my chest, wondering how often Mother had cowered before men like this, how she escaped . . . if I would escape.

"What's this?" A large hand shot toward me and took hold of the parchment.

"No," I protested weakly. "This is mine."

"I don't think it can be yours, little woman. You didn't come in with it, and everything here belongs to me." A sinful smile spread on his lips as he ran his eyes over me.

I struggled to keep hold of my drawing, but the man would have torn it if I hadn't surrendered my grip. He looked at the parchment. "My balance ledger, and an old one at that. How can this interest you?" Then, he turned the parchment over and saw the drawing on the back. "More than just a lady of the shadows, I see." His lips curled derisively. "Well, I think we'll call this an even trade, then. Your company for the use of my good parchment."

I shook my head, more to deny what he called me than to turn down his offer. My bones again felt chilled.

He proffered the drawing toward me, looking down his long arm at me as I curled into a corner of his home. I lifted a hand to receive the only payment I wanted. Just as I was about to take it, he whipped the drawing away and ripped it into several pieces. With a sinking feeling, I watched the delight on his face as he destroyed the small drawing. I cowered in his shadow, my feet and legs pulled tightly against my chest as the entire night flashed in my mind with terrible vividness.

When he finished, he dropped the scraps to the floor. "I will keep my ledger. Your payment is where I left it. Go."

Unable to stand or walk, I crawled to the door. I looked back at the heap of torn parchment on the floor, the fire, my blackened stick, and finally at the man who now busied himself across the room. No further thought had he for me, or for what he had done. Quietly, I reached up, took his meager offering and stole home with my payment.

The ground scraped roughly at the palms of my hands and my knees and toes, but I did not trust my muscles to carry me upright. Across the cold ground I went, slinking home, only because I could think of no place else to go.

At our lintel I knocked, feeling foreign to my own home. When the door swung open, I saw Mother's knowing eyes. She helped me in, sat me by the fire, and placed a woolen blanket over my shoulders. Without a word she pried my rigid fingers from around the fistful of coins and dropped them into a small leather purse which she carefully stowed in a hollow beneath the rug.

As I tried to regain some warmth, she busied herself with supper. I noticed something that I never had before: she made no sound with her feet when she moved. The very movements of her arms swept in slow, silent arcs that did not rustle her garments. Only the tap of the knife's blade against the cutting board. The slip of vegetables into the water of our pot. The hiss and crackle of fire. Even the clink of bowls and cups being set at the table. But she made no impression on the world, left no imprint. I lost myself in wonder as to whether she chose it so, or if all the world had left her behind, unremembered.

We ate bone-broth that night, mild slurps in the half-light of our small fire. Something had forever changed between us. I spent most of those late hours searching for a stick to char on the coals, so I could recreate my sketch.

When mother died, I found enough money to pay for her burial with little more than enough left to survive a week on my own. Those first days after she had gone, I mourned the only friend I had ever had, the only parent, the only kind touch. As the week passed, however, I thought of her with less affection. Why had she not taught me to be more than she had become?

In life, she had been a kind woman, though ignorant. She had made her way by walking the streets in search of company. It was not a good way to earn a living. Some days were more brutal than others. I learned that awful truth one night when mother crept through the door with bruises marking her cheeks.

She had sat beside our hearth, her face drawn. I brought a bowl of water and a cloth, and dabbed at the dried blood. Mother turned vacant eyes upon me, as I washed her battered face. She had seated herself in the same chair she would place me the night I crawled home after my sketch had been torn by that man's rough hands. The same hearthstones cradled embers on both nights, separated by years of fireside washings. The same world spoke with its awful voice of judgement, indifference and derision, drawing us together in our hut near the quarry.

Looking deep into my eyes, Mother said, "Once you allow your feet upon a path, others are not so quick to let you take another."

Mother once had a pretty face. But in time, it grew rutted with scars from the rough clients she sometimes knew.

Sometime before she died, I stopped washing her face for her.

I did cleanse her cheeks and brow a final time, though, when I prepared her for the grave. When she had been laid to rest, I locked myself in our small home near the quarry and fashioned a drawing of the face that swept me away from the world I lived in. Rendering the image became my only solace; the smell of smoking wood a salve to my fragile emotions.

My reputation did not spread quickly. I took care to conceal myself, and discretion by those who came to my hut served me well. Had it not been so, Ishmael might never have spoken to me.

Drawing water at the well near the base of the quarry one day, a hand took my heavy pitcher from me and hoisted it atop broad shoulders. When I turned, I beheld the handsomest face I had ever seen.

"Fair hands should be spared such work," the young man said, grinning. "And I should make myself a goat were I to watch you toil and not lend my aid."

I demurred, glancing around to see if anyone who might recognize me was nearby. I relaxed, returning the smile. "I am not helpless."

The man shook his head. "That is not what I said." He smiled. "I am Ishmael." A subtle upward lilt in his name intimated his desire to know my name.

"Rebekah," I answered. "And I have drawn my own water for a long time."

"Then I have missed a thousand opportunities to preserve your delicate hands." He surprised me by taking a gentle hold of the tips of my fingers. He studied them with affected interest, making quizzical sounds deep in his throat.

Amused, a laugh escaped me. "They are not so . . . delicate," I finally replied. "They are the hands of a woman who works, and are not in immediate need of rescue."

He arched a brow. "And quick with her tongue. You should be careful not to steal my heart so fast. There's delight in slow acquaintance." He let go my hand. "I've not seen you here before, but I do not come near the city often. I could to with some conversation."

Eager eyes awaited my reply. I felt danger in openly speaking to anyone, but I could not find the strength to stop. The only eyes that held my gaze longer belonged to those in my sketches. It seemed the very look of me either frightened or disgusted the people I passed upon the street. The meager acknowledgement in simply being looked at, eye to eye, came to me like the sweetest wine. Conversation, and what seemed genuine interest in me, made my blood race. I could hear the pulse of my heart, and hoped I did not appear over-eager.

"I am very busy," I lied. "But I might make time to talk with you more."

One corner of his mouth hooked into a grin. "When?"

"Tomorrow," I answered. "Here. I'll need more water." I walked away, trying not to rush in my excitement. With my back to him, a smile spread across my face so wide that the muscles in my cheeks ached.

For weeks we met at the well near the base of the quarry. We talked. Often, we walked, Ishmael carrying my pitcher upon his shoulder. He was a shepherd, and smelled faintly of his flock. But as the days passed, I dreamed that he hoisted our child there, and that we strolled in the morning sun with our family as other people do.

A NIGHT OF PEACE

For a time, it was Ishmael's face I tried to draw by my fire when the men left my hut. With my charred sticks I crafted his nose and cheeks, and secretly knew I would prove Mother wrong about my life's path. Each night before going to sleep, I placed my pitcher and a sketch near the door, readied for my early visit to the well . . . and Ishmael. Ready, myself, to blush at his compliments over my drawings, and admire the strength in his shoulders.

On a bright morning, shadows still long from a low eastern sun, I approached the well and saw my friend sitting with hunched shoulders. I considered turning back; whatever had happened I did not want to know. I desperately needed to preserve this precious slice of happiness. I should return again tomorrow, and Ishmael would be standing tall again, with his broad shoulders prepared to carry my pitcher.

But he was my friend, and the love I felt for him overshadowed my personal concerns. Something oppressed him. I could sense it. Years of sharing the hut with Mother had taught me what defeat looked like in the body of another.

I came up beside him and stood unnoticed a moment before speaking. "Hello."

Ishmael jumped. "You startled me. I did not hear you."

I offered a smile. "Did you not sleep well?" I tried to speak casually.

"No," he murmured.

"Were you up late with wine and song?" I lent a hint of humor to my words. I placed the pitcher beside him but he did not reach to assist me.

"No," he repeated. "I . . ." He looked up at me, then quickly away. "I heard some things . . ."

The pounding in my head came in deafening waves. Somewhere beneath the delusion I had anticipated this moment. But so far down had I hidden my secret from him, that it came to me as a shock.

I considered denying everything, or simply playing ignorant. I could do neither convincingly. I turned squarely toward Ishmael, hoping he would look at me. He did not.

"You say nothing." His voice quavered with emotion. "It is as good as an answer."

He struggled with something. I waited, feeling scrutinized and low, but hoping that what we had been building would endure even this. I wanted him to regard me as I know he did that first day, and believe the better part of who I was. The silence between us stretched. I began to mourn the loss of him while standing still in his company. No greater loneliness have I ever felt.

"Why did you not tell me?" His words were a husk, both ire and sadness.

I reached to take his hand. He recoiled. "I did," I implored. "All that we shared is true. The rest is the hardness of the world. Something I bear alone . . . and could beat with a strong pair of shoulders." I reached again, deciding I loved him with a certainty I hadn't accepted until that very moment. Always before I had seen understanding in the lines at the corners of his eyes and mouth. Today, the taut pull of having been betrayed held in his countenance, and would not be softened. I dropped my hand to my side and turned to look at the empty water pitcher.

"Goodbye." He walked back toward Bethlehem.

As he disappeared in the distance, I wept silent tears both for him and for the words he first said to me when I arrived at the well:

"You startled me, I did not hear you." I had truly become just like Mother, passing through this world and leaving no trace, no impression, behind.

That night my sketches could produce only one form, and it remained so for a very long time.

Always I drew the same face. It was a child, a beautiful boy child. I think he was the image of what I had hoped my son would be if my life had been different. And always I rolled the drawings together in a thick scroll and hid it safely in the shadows beneath my bed.

Though the instruments of my simple art were coarse, the soot from the fire made a soft and thoughtful portrait of this child I would never know. I purchased used parchment from the tradesmen in town, making use of the back sides of their ledgers and epistles. With time, I began to cherish the particular look and feel of the sketches I made. While I might have afforded some charcoal or ink, instead I struck a bargain with a local carpenter named Luke to haul away piles of unusable wood. In return, I kept from the scraps, the lengths of wood shaped into hand-sized rods, which I used in my art.

Needing some new materials, one day I visited the carpenter to see what I could salvage. As I approached the man's work benches, I found him cradling his face in his large, calloused hands.

Cautiously, I approached. Scanning the ground around his work area, I saw little indication that he'd done much work of late. One pile did lay against the far wall. Amidst shavings and chips, small figurines of animals and people lay at odd angles. A toy or two also lay broken in the scrap, including a carving of a castle with slender pieces now snapped and broken. Strewn about these other items were several pieces that would suit me well.

In deference, I paused before him. "Hello."

He raised his head and stared vacantly at me, not answering.

"Is it all right for me to take the wood?" I bowed slightly, feeling suddenly scrutinized, though his eyes held no malice.

So slight that from a greater distance I might not have seen it, the carpenter shook his head.

My heart dropped. I could use any stick, surely, but the drawings I made with the wood I retrieved from beneath his benches was far superior, fitting my hand more efficiently, the charred ends spreading soot more evenly as I traced my lines.

Quickly I made my plea. "If I have offended you, please let me make it right. I will do whatever you say. I'll sweep the grounds. I'll wash your tools."

As if shaken from sleep, the carpenter's eyes suddenly became alert. His head shook in earnest. "Why shouldn't you have them?" he replied, sarcasm lilting in his voice. He turned and pointed at the meager scrap pile. "Take them away. The pitiful waste judges me in its scarcity. Our deal is that you take them for free, is it not?" He snorted. "That is my usual wage, as well. I'm glad to do business with you, dear lady."

I had never seen the carpenter so troubled. I did not know what ills had beset him, but his words frightened me. I suffered one last look at the bits of wood, then turned and started home.

A few steps had I taken, when Luke called out, "Wait!"

I halted, half-turning toward him. The carpenter stood, and went to the pile of scraps. He picked up several of the best pieces from the shavings and leftovers and brought them to me.

"Take them," he offered. "I've no need of them."

Gently, he placed them in my hands, putting the broken castle on top. I thanked him, then added, "But I should take the shavings and waste with me."

"Not today," he said.

Regret seemed to weigh heavily upon him. Or perhaps worry; I knew his wife was with child. Work was clearly not abundant, and his tables were probably empty.

I resisted the urge to assure him with a touch. Instead, I spoke briefly. "You have your wife and child. You are rich."

He shut his eyes against my words. "Yes, if they are not stripped from me by the harshness of these times, and this world."

I had no comfort to give him, and left believing that with a different face misery visits everyone.

That night, as the sun fell behind the horizon, I waited as I always did for a knock on the door of my hut.

On that night, no one came.

A quiet stillness stretched out and nary a tap sounded at my lintel. I finally left the confines of the hut and went to the edge of the quarry to breathe the night air and think again of how I might have had a different life. My sins weighed heavily upon me, and I longed for the peace of the grave.

At the edge of the quarry, overlooking a cavernous hole, I gazed up into a vast night, deep and violet and calm. I saw a bright star, glowing like the embers in my fire. It was the first night since the loss of my childhood that I was alone and free to dream my dreams and forget.

While the world slept, and with my unseemly business unattended for a night, I imagined a different life. I imagined what I would name the babe in my drawings, and dreamed myself away from the sweat and candle stench of my shack at the foot of the stone mount. Once more I imagined the scenes in my drawings, believing they could one day be real: a child in the large and gentle hands of a father whose face I never had imagination enough to draw.

I do not know how long I stood there. In the glow of that night star I basked and felt normal, even wistful. And in my mind, the image of the child came with insistence and greater clarity than ever before.

Beneath the gleam of that star, I hastened back to my hut and removed the sticks that were my drawing instruments from beneath the bed. Gently, I pulled a few of the pillars from the carpenter's wooden castle and placed them at the edge of the coals to char. When they were ready, I took a piece of parchment from my chest and began a new sketch. I made broad strokes and subtle changes. I drew careful lines and intelligent eyes. I placed the child in swaddling clothes and cradled in the arms of a slight, but tender young woman. This time I drew the face of that woman, replicating there my own face, daring just once to look into the hope of my inmost heart since losing Ishmael.

Morning dawned before the sketch was done, but I was not the least tired. As sunshine stole through the cracks in my hut, I rolled the sketch and stowed it beneath my bed. Moments later, I heard a commotion outside as the great drunkard—"James of the Cask" we called him—ran at a break-neck pace through the roads, announcing the birth of a messiah. I knew of the prophecies, but had long since lost my belief in a savior. None could save such as I.

Still, it was hard not to desire the message to be true. As I had stood at the edge of the quarry, watching the night becalmed of wind and without the memory of my past, had I not wished upon that star to be saved from myself? I shut my eyes and recalled the great star, like the embers in my fire that produce the implement of my art. I had been given a night of peace, a night to believe in my dream, in redemption from all I was. I had sat up all night crafting an image of the future I hoped for, and I had been given the most wonderful gift I could have imagined for myself: a night of peace. I decided I must meet this babe.

I put on my shawl and prepared to leave. Hesitating, I stopped and took my newest sketch from beneath my bed. I cut a length of my hair, tied the parchment closed, and set off into town.

It took me only moments to learn of a man and woman who had been put up in the stable of an inn where poor travelers to Bethlehem often stayed. I walked there with growing excitement, hoping to see the newborn child.

As I drew close to a small group of people at the entrance of the hillside stable, I paused, not daring to enter, for fear that those who had come might know me and disapprove of my presence. Tears were rolling down my cheeks, because I wanted to thank the child for the previous night's gift: a peaceful moment in which I had forgotten who I was and considered what I wanted to be. But my feet would not move, and I stood frozen in the morning sun, afraid to walk or speak lest I draw attention to myself.

The crowd suddenly parted. A strong young man led a beautiful young lady out of the stable, a girl my own age holding a child close to her chest. They made their way past the well-wishers toward the rear entrance of the inn. The man and woman came close to me and had nearly passed before pausing and turning toward me.

I could not look into their eyes. My shame fell upon me like a thousand stones from the quarry, and I dropped to my knees.

The young man knelt beside me and called his wife to kneel as well. The young mother shifted the child to one arm, and put her free hand upon my chin, lifting my head. The crowd came round to watch, keeping a respectful distance.

"This is my son," she said, proffering the child toward me. With tentative hands, I reached for him, and cradled his tiny head in the crook of my arm. My tears fell upon his ruddy cheeks. I softly wiped them away, hoping his mother would not take him back from my arms. A lasting moment of awareness and love enveloped me.

This child.

His was the face in my sketch.

This was the likeness I had crafted time and time again to soothe my heart when the burdens of my guilt grew too heavy.

Still holding the child, I drew the parchment from my robe and handed it to the mother. She gently untied the lock of hair and unrolled the drawing. To my surprise, her eyes welled with tears.

"It's lovely," she whispered, "You know, you and I look very much alike."

I looked intently into her eyes and saw no guile. When my surprise ebbed, I saw that she was right.

"I will keep your picture always, and show it to when he is grown," the woman said. "It is a wonderful talent you have."

We knelt for several more moments, sharing a silence over the child. When they took their leave, I stood, began walking in the opposite direction of my hut, and never looked back.

A Potter's Clay

My papa taught me to use the clay when I was six; my hands shook even then.

"Place your hands on it gently, but firmly, Anna," he instructed. It was the first time he had given me a portion of clay to mold.

I reached for it with trepidation, and knocked the lump from the table. Expecting to hear his impatient reproach, my hands shook more violently than usual, and I tried to calm them by knitting my fingers tightly together.

Papa looked at me, bent to pick up the clay, and took hold of my hands. He tenderly pried my fingers apart and placed the clay in my palm. "Squeeze it for a while, dear. Just roll and flatten it and squeeze it until it is warm." He then went about his work on the wheel.

My hands continued to shake. They always did. But I followed his directions and found that I liked the feel of the soft pliable substance in my hands and fingers. I even liked the way it got under my nails. I rolled it between my palms, pressed my knuckles into it, poked my fingers through it. The clay held the wonderful smell of promise, permanence, of shapes and implements waiting to be discovered. It yielded to my touch, never accusing my clumsy fingers. It forgave my unsteadiness with the same latent promise felt by everyone who took clay in hand.

"You're getting it," Papa said, somehow able to watch me without averting his eyes from his work. "Keep at it. Persistence is rewarded when one makes use of her hands." He shot me a glance. "There's no hurry, dear. Each time you finish, you'll have learned something new."

"You think I could make things as beautiful as you, Papa?"

"Sweet one," he said, lowering a loving gaze, "I've no doubt you'll one day craft more glorious items than mine. And do you know what?"

"What?"

He motioned me close. I put down my clay and drew up beside him. He gave me a conspiratorial wink before wrapping me in a firm hug. I smiled over his shoulder, grasped his wide belly, and squeezed him back. "You see, when you're holding someone tight, your hands don't shake."

Papa was right. The realization of it persuaded me right then to follow him as a potter. By the time he had finished his vase, I had created a cup of my own. I wrote my name in the side and set it on the table. It did not stand straight, but it was mine, and Papa kissed me on the forehead when he saw it.

"You will be a wonderful potter one day, Anna. Do not let your hands fool you. You have the soul of a creator, the desire of an artist." He put my cup on the shelf with his wonderful plates and bowls, and we went to the kitchen to share some grapes.

Papa died when I was twelve, but by then I was capable of making sellable vases and bowls. They were not as beautiful as his, but our shop had a reputation at the market, and I always made enough for Mother and I to eat. Three years later, to my sorrow, she went to her rest beside Papa. I had been their only child. I went on shaping the clay.

A few years later, I stopped going out into the crowded market, because I could never sufficiently hide my hands. They always quaked more when I was nervous. The market is not the place for an anxious merchant. So I had a display shelf built in my home, and between my papa's reputation, and my own work, I earned a steady clientele who purchased my wares by visiting me where I lived and worked.

But living alone, unwilling to leave the house, I had no prospects for marriage. I learned how differently a man regarded me when I saw the way he looked at other women. Soon I lost my youth. And older women seldom marry. I told myself time did not allow it, as I was always crafting another piece to sell. With age, I admitted to myself that blaming my loneliness on my work was a lie.

When I forgot the truth, there were always reminders.

One day, Nehemiah and Alma came to my home to purchase a number of vases. They had become my best customers by buying my work to sell to the homes of the king's highest advisors. Busy cleaning in the back room, I did not immediately hear them. Once I heard their voices, I paused to listen.

"She does make fine work," Alma said.

"That she does. I believe her skill is nearly equal to her father's," agreed Nehemiah.

I smiled to myself at the compliment, then suddenly felt awkward, listening to a private conversation. Rarely did I hear honest opinions about my work, and I enjoyed the sound of men in my home, even though they were there as customers. They did not know I could hear them, so I kept still a moment to enjoy the praise that people are often unwilling to share openly.

Alma's footsteps plodded across the room. "The remarkable thing is that she is able to accomplish such fine work with those hands of hers. Have you seen them?"

There was no answer and I assumed Nehemiah nodded.

"They are frightful. I believe she is diseased, somehow. It is not natural for a woman to have such a condition." His voice grew hushed, but in my small home a whisper carried to every corner.

"Has she always had such unsteady hands?" asked Nehemiah.

"Always," Alma whispered, as if suddenly afraid of being overheard.

Nehemiah spoke quietly, too. "It is a shame she must be alone with such an ailment. But her work seems profitable." I heard something being lifted from my display shelf. I imagined Nehemiah inspecting a piece of my work. "Who would ever guess that she could fashion such fine things? One would marry an asset by taking her to wife."

"Yes, you are right, of course, but what man would have her?" Alma's tone became softer still. "It may be that her illness would pass along to her children. No father wants a son whose hands flutter about, a son who may not be able to hold fast his tools or purse. Her table is attended by empty chairs," he observed, dragging one out and sitting heavily upon it. "I'll play guest to her."

Nehemiah stifled a chortle. "I am glad she can sustain herself, because she is not likely to find a husband who will tolerate such . . . unsteadiness."

I heard him replace the withdrawn item to its place on the display shelf. Standing in my workroom I looked at my hands, now shaking violently. They were right. I had never allowed myself to say it aloud, but I had always known. To fashion the clay I had used my hands well, but they were a curse in every other endeavor of life. I pressed them roughly into my eyes, forcing back the tears. When I had regained my composure, I hid my hands in my dress and went to service my best customers.

After that day I spent more hours at my wheel. I worked harder to create beautiful pieces to sell. I awoke well before dawn and worked with the clay until I had need to light my lamp. After supper I continued until my arms grew heavy and weary. As time passed, the lines in the vases and pots and bowls I made became more elegant, the designs etched into their sides more pleasing. In the years that followed, my work became renowned throughout Bethlehem. Jacob the tradesman, who ran the market, even purchased some of my finer pieces to sell into other cities of Judaea. Some could even be found in the halls at Herod's court. And Abraham, who supplied me with my clay, told me of rumors and myths the people had created about me, because I was never seen out in the street. Some thought I was a witch. Some thought I had a special appointment from Yahweh. Others simply considered me strange and unfriendly. Abraham and I laughed together about their speculation; he was the closest thing I had to a friend.

My hands shook more each passing year. My fingers stiffened, and molding the clay became more difficult. I fretted the day I would no longer be able to support myself with my work. Still, I was at peace, for I was resigned to my solitude, and I always had the warmth of the clay beneath my fingers.

When I finally took to using a walking stick to get around my home, I decided I would make my finest vase, a testimony to the work of my life, and to my Papa. It would be my most permanent thing, an object of beauty that belied the infirmity of my hands. I began the project, because I also knew my time to join Papa was near. I prayed my hands would be calm in the next life. In the meantime I wanted to create one last great work, my best attempt at fashioning something beautiful to leave behind. However long it took, it would be magnificent.

I used the long hours after supper to refine my design, working elaborate grooves and soft but grand curves into the clay. By the light of the oil, I labored and put my unquiet hands to use in what I was sure would be the most beautiful vessel created in this life.

Many times I came to an impasse, knowing I hadn't got it right. I would scrap the work and begin again. The strength in my hands lasted in decreasing durations each passing week. I began to worry I might not finish the vase at all. I wanted more than anything to do this one thing, but it had to be perfect.

Before bed each night I rubbed my hands with olive oil blended with cayenne and peppermint. Seated at my supper table, I stared at my display shelves, smelling the soothing herbs on my hands, and feeling the curse and blessing of my trembling extremities. I had learned patience and persistence from them, but I had also learned anxiety and isolation.

Then, one evening, the piece was done. I hadn't thought I was close, but suddenly I slowed the wheel and looked at the vase. It was as perfect as I could make it. There seemed to be nothing left for me to do, so I hobbled to my bed and fell onto it, taking no time for my ointment. The next day, once the pot had cooled from the fire, I carefully placed the vase in my bedroom chest and went back to making bowls.

I thought myself empty after the vase rested safe and complete. I felt I had nothing more to contribute.

Again life reminded me of larger truths.

A year passed, maybe more. I cannot count how many bowls I made. My hands became like thick butterflies at the end of arms that seemed disconnected from me, even when I worked at the clay. At night, sleep eluded me as my hands twisted and writhed upon my bedding—the herbs no longer helped to soothe them. Long hours of night passed as I wondered what life might be like with carefree hands. I felt every pulse of my heart through the engorged veins of my wrists. The lines in my palms ached. I imagined how I would end up, beating at doors for alms with numb fists.

I welcomed the dawn. It gave me a place to put my hands again, forcing them to create, produce.

In the twilight of dawn on one particular morning, I took some bread to eat and ambled to my workroom. I sat upon my stool and pulled back the wet cloth that covered my clay. With great effort, I drew a lump and dropped it on the wheel where I could begin. Heaving a sigh, I flexed my fingers, wincing at the pain. My hands trembled in great swinging arcs, making full quarter-turns in the air. With desperation I dropped them on the clay and closed my eyes. *Another bowl. Just one more.* I repeated the same incantation every morning.

I opened my eyes and tried to begin. Nothing happened. My fingers moved, but with less coordination than was necessary to perform their function. I paused, shook them, and started again. Nothing. The clay beneath my hands felt as though I touched it through a heavy drape. The warmth, the promise I'd grown to love in the clay could not be felt. I could see my hands on it, watched my fingers writhe in a semblance of creative motion, but they would not respond to the need I desired of them.

For hours I tried to make them behave. For hours I sat in frustration, pushing cumbersome fists and fingers into the clay. My ability to create was gone, though everything else remained the same: the desire, the need, and the clay itself. Even the smell remained, that beautiful scent of pliable clay. A pungent reminder and insult to the loss of this most wonderful, yet basic and simple task.

Finally, I lifted my hands before my eyes and knew in despair that they had become as useful to me as stone or wood. They might well have been fashioned of clay for as much feeling as I had in them. As the day wore on, I watched the lump of clay dry on my wheel, its promise slowly dying as it became hard, cracked, inflexible. I had thought I was empty, that there could be nothing more for me once my exquisite vase was finished. But that day I sat and mourned a piece of clay that would never become a bowl. I sat and mourned myself.

I continued to mourn as my shelves emptied of inventory.

In the weeks that followed, I sat at my table and watched as customers purchased what remained of my work. Bowls, vases, pitchers, all slowly disappeared, leaving the display shelves barren. As I rested my useless hands in my lap, I stared at the vacancies there that I could no longer fill. They mocked me. Every purchase left more space and less stock that would go unreplenished. The void created there was like a wide, toothless grin, smiling its mockery at me.

When I could suffer it no more, I made arrangements for the shelves to be removed. I wanted no reminder of the life I'd known, the simple pleasure of crafting a bowl from clay.

The man that came to dismantle the shelves worked quietly, inspecting the wood as he placed it in neat piles on the floor.

After one wall had been cleared, the carpenter approached me tentatively. "Will you want to keep the wood?"

I looked past him at the shelves that had allowed me to work and live at home, avoiding the questions and anxiety I'd experienced in the market. All I could see was my own inability to create. "No, take it far from here, young man. It is sore for me to look upon."

"May I keep it in trade for my services?" A hopeful expression raised his brow. "I've work that may require it. I'll be glad to take it all from here and charge you nothing."

Considering his request, I thought I might have had some reservations about my display shelves being remade into something else. Instead, I felt nothing. "Do as you please. They have no value for me anymore."

The carpenter offered a weak smile, and went back to his work. Shortly, the few bowls I had left sat on the floor in the corner.

Yet even with the shelving gone, I continued to mourn until the night Abraham came by unannounced.

"Anna, get up, get up!" He cried, knocking on my door.

"What is it?" I grumped, taking up my walking stick.

"I know how unhappy you've been, but I have something to tell you that may brighten your mood." He knocked at the door again to hasten me.

I lit the lamp and limped to the door. Abraham, hearing me from without, started talking before I had even unfastened the latch, his voice strident.

"It's happened, Anna! The messiah has arrived! Come as a child and born in a stable. Put on your shoes and let us go. He lies just moments away. I've been to see him; he is beautiful. Hurry!" He paused to take a breath.

"Our Christ? He is here? In Bethlehem?" I opened the door with difficulty and swept it back with my shoulder.

"Yes. Yes! Now, no more talk, come!" Abraham tried to grab my elbow, but I shifted out of reach. "Do you not want to greet him?" my friend asked with incredulity.

"How do you know it is he?" I leaned heavily upon my walking stick, my legs weak with the sudden rise from bed.

"Step out into the street, will you!" he demanded.

I did as he asked and looked where he pointed into the sky at a fabulous star.

"Come on! Let us go together." He again tried to take my arm, reaching hastily to assist me.

I hit his leg with my walking stick. "I will come, but I have something to do first. Where is he?"

Abraham shook his head, irritated. "Fine. But hurry! Just follow the star." Then he was swiftly gone toward the end of the street, disappearing in the shadows.

I looked again at the grand star. *Perhaps this is why I hadn't passed this life yet. Why I've remained here with my useless hands.* I went inside, straight to my chest. I wrapped my unsteady fingers around my special vase and lifted it out. I would give the child this thing, the most beautiful item I had ever made with my diseased hands. I hugged the vase close to my bosom and set out after Abraham.

The night was calm, almost reverent. The luminous glow of the star touched my vase on its delicate edges. Slowly, I hobbled through town with my walking stick, following the light to the gathering at a stable.

Surprised looks greeted me. A few of the younger people had never seen me, but seemed to know who I was just the same. They parted, allowing me to move to the front of the crowd.

Oil lamps lit the stable with warm, golden hues. It still smelled of stable animals, but no one seemed to mind. A few feet beyond the last attendants, a man and woman knelt beside a feed-box, which held an infant wrapped tightly in swaddling clothes.

Uncertainly, I crept forward, taking great care not to jostle my vase or lose my grip. I turned my back to people as I passed them, afraid a sudden movement might pry my precious cargo loose. But no one contended with me, and I came easily to the front of the onlookers.

There I stood in awe, looking at the young couple and the babe. A fine family, poor to be sure, but resolute somehow. I appreciated the quiet determination beneath their humility; I had learned it well. Then I gazed on the child. It occurred to me a little odd to see redemption lying in a manger, but the thought passed quickly, replaced by a certainty I could not explain. A gentle spirit rested in the stable, and I could only think of my first hopeful attempt to create a cup, and the kiss it had earned me from my Papa. With that thought, my loneliness left me, and I nodded in understanding to no one in particular.

Around the manger many things had been laid, some extravagant, others less so. I searched the mother's eyes for permission to present my gift. She nodded, and I stooped forward. I extended my vase to place it near the manger. In that moment, my hands shook violently. I tightened my grip, but my hands would not respond. A weak groan escaped my lips as I fought my own infirmity to preserve this cherished gift of mine. The vase tottered, my fingers weakened. In an instant I lost my grip. The delicate vase fell to the ground.

The straw where my vase fell was thin, the ground beneath it hard. The vase shattered with a splintery pop and pieces fell in a pile at the foot of the manger. I looked down at the rubble in disbelief. It was ruined, my life's work. The greatest monument created by my poor hands. I pushed my quavering fingers against my eyes and turned away from the child.

A hand rested on my shoulder. I nearly pulled away, thinking it to be Abraham again, always the one to console. But the hand was soft. I lowered my arms and looked into the face of the child's mother. In her other hand she held a piece of my vase.

"It is beautiful." She let go of my arm and traced one of the thin lines across the surface of the fragment she held. "You have the hands of a creator."

"No, dear woman . . ." I began, but was unable to finish the thought.

The woman returned to the manger, handing the piece of my vase to her husband. She leaned down to her son, lifted him from his bed of straw, and came back to where I stood.

The child was beautiful, peaceful.

His mother extended him toward me.

I shook my head. "I cannot. My hands are unsteady and weak. It is not safe."

"Please, I would like you to hold my son. Let him know of the care in those same hands that made this vase you brought tonight to honor him." The lady did not retreat.

Slowly, I lifted my trembling hands toward the child.

"His name is Jeshua," she offered.

My hands shook and trembled violently, but I put them under the babe and pulled him to my bosom. As I held the infant, I felt his warmth and thought of the clay, and cradled him with kindness and strength and surety. *When you're holding someone tight, your hands don't shake*. My eyes grew wet, and I spared a look at his mother.

"Thank you," I whispered.

She smiled and returned to sit with her husband.

And I did not grow weak, but held the baby fast. My hands did not tremble or quake, but knew, at last, the greatest beauty of creation.

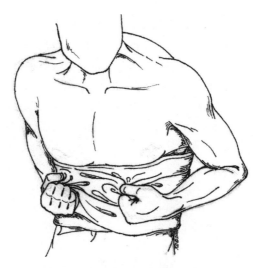

Swaddling Clothes

In the streets of my childhood, I wore loose clothes to hide my hump, and struggled to stand straight like the other children. The effort exhausted me. And never so much as when I tried to run. The shape of my spine hindered my legs, and I scuttled along after the other children, soon falling too far behind the pack to find them.

But one time I did catch up.

In a small square near the synagogue the children had stopped to continue a game of tag. Passersby grumbled as the youngsters maneuvered around them, using them as barriers. I watched near the wall, glad to listen to the bright peals of delighted screams echoing off the stone. I could not move as quickly as the rest, but just being close made me feel a part of the game.

The children's sandals clapped rhythmic songs. Dust stirred, lifting with it chaff into the strong fall of sun. I leaned against the wall, supporting myself against the merciless, earthward pull that pained my back. I realized I didn't belong amongst the other children. We were the same age, but I already felt old, past the innocence of youth. I watched with older eyes and knew my stoop had taught me adulthood much too soon. The moment of reflection passed, washed under by the yelps and laughter of children fleeing one another in mad sprints.

At one point, Benjamin, the group leader, rushed in front of a man leading a mule laden with several baskets. The man bristled with reproach. "A pox upon you, boy! The street isn't for games. Find yourself somewhere else to play!"

Seeing the man's reaction, I felt relieved that perhaps there *was* something different in the way I watched the others play, different from adult eyes. Perhaps I wasn't as old inside as I felt. The man shook his head disapprovingly and tugged the reins of his mule to continue on his way. He trudged down the street, his shoulders hunched as though drawn earthward from the weight of unseen responsibility. I ignored the similarity of our backs and laughed as I turned back to the children.

"What are you laughing at, Jeremiah?" Benjamin chided. "That snail of a man is twice as fast as you are, even dragging his mule." He assumed a threatening stance and glared at me. The others fell in behind him, the game now suspended. "He may be sour, but he knows the color of the sky by looking up." Benjamin hit his friend Joel in the chest with the back of his hand, and the two laughed in unison.

I wanted to back away, scuttle down the wall and disappear into the next street. But the children soon came around me, hemming me in. "I meant nothing by it, Ben," I stammered. "I thought it was funny how you made him rear up." I tried to smile and hide my growing panic.

"Is that right?" Benjamin mocked. "Well, maybe we can do the same for you. Straighten you out."

I cowered closer to the wall, pressing my cheek against the rough stone. I wanted something to cling to, but nothing was at hand.

With a sudden gleam in his eye, Benjamin rushed over to Julia and tore a large doll from her hands. In an instant, he had loosed the swaddling from around the doll and looped it in his fist. Following his lead, a second girl unclothed her own toy doll, and proffered the swaddling toward me with a strange grin.

"I don't understand." I looked around at every face, aware that each wore a similar, strange and expectant smile. My heart thrummed in my chest. Whatever wisdom I thought I shared with adults fled me; I had no idea what they meant to do. I cowered against the wall.

"Don't worry, Jeremiah, we're going to help you," Ben assured me. He stepped back into the street and bade me follow him.

I wonder sometimes what might have been different if I'd stayed close to the rock wall. I wonder if the smallest hopes I kept that others would look beyond my hump were more pitiful than the hump itself. But I took hesitant steps into the street, trying to watch each child from my stoop . . . hoping Ben meant what he said.

"What do you mean, Ben? How are you going to help me?" I stopped, aware that the circle had closed behind me, feet stirring more dust and chaff.

"Did your mother bathe you in salted water when you were born, Jeremiah? Did she wrap you tight so that you'd grow straight and strong?" One side of his mouth lifted in a snarling grin. "You see, I think she did not. And each anniversary of your birth you grow more crooked, more hunched back to the smell of dirt and dung, and further from the light Eternal Father placed in the sky . . . Further from Yahweh himself."

"What do you mean? Why should I—"

Benjamin pounced, circling me so fast I scarcely had time to do more than breathe. Around he went again, binding me with the swaddling. Julia joined him, and the children began to dance around me, some laughing, others chanting verses of song. Before I could think to untangle myself, I was bound too tightly to get away. From other hands, more swaddling appeared. The harder I struggled, the tighter the strips of cloth held me fast.

My legs weakened, threatening to collapse me to my knees. I did not want to give them that satisfaction. I stood strong, weaving but never falling, as they wrapped me up with the swaddling. I called out, but my words were too weak to rise above the din. My vision blurred, hot tears came unbidden and scorched my cheeks as I strained against the bands.

"Come on, he's had enough," one of the boys called. I looked up and saw Luke disengaged from the mob. "Stop it," he repeated. When he tried to pull Benjamin from the swirl, the group leader turned and hit him in the face. Luke fled, perhaps to get help.

SWADDLING CLOTHES

I coughed and choked from the dust rising off the ground. My sputtering words and cries drew more laughter from the ring of children who pranced around me. My back began to cramp. I knew I would soon fall. I feared they might kick me or stomp on me. Distorted mouths swam in and out of view as I tried to fix my sight on something to steady myself without the use of my arms. The sounds of ridicule and the stench of my own panic entered my senses as through a filter. My mind retreated far away from the insults, like holding my breath underwater and listening to children splash and play at the water's surface. When I could take no more, a deep voice broke the barrier of my own barricade, bellowing from up the street. The children dispersed abruptly, their laughter following them in diminishing echoes.

The sudden silence came like an incrimination. Before the owner of the voice could come to my aid, I hobbled away as fast as I could, still unable to free myself from the swaddling.

When I knew the danger was past, I slowed, replaying the attack over and over again in my mind. Something nagged at me. I finally stopped and concentrated so I could find out what. There was something I should have done . . . "Blue," I finally muttered in reply to Ben's accusation that I could not see the color of the sky. "The sky is blue . . ." I looked around at a perplexed elderly woman who stared at me. With that, I slouched toward home.

When I arrived, my legs gave out. I fell through the door and was picked up by strong, tender hands. I closed my eyes as a wet cloth wiped my face and hands. Then the swaddling began to loosen.

Without opening my eyes I asked, "Mother, did you not salt or swaddle me when I was born? Is that why I bear this hump and walk bent over?"

Silence followed, and I knew the children had been right. I struggled to look up. My only friend's eyes were glossy with tears. She opened her mouth to say something, but closed it again without uttering a word. After several moments she gained a little composure and said simply, "I was young, Jeremiah, and your father was taken back to Yahweh by illness before you were born. I had no money, and you came while I was half a day's walk from Bethlehem. There was no one to help me. It is a miracle you survived at all." She paused, perhaps hoping to hear my forgiveness. I said nothing. "I am sorry," she finished. Then she touched my cheek and rushed from the room, leaving me with the revelation that my Eternal Father was not responsible for my twisted body.

I bent over the swaddling that had bound me, and clutched them in my hands until the bones ached in my fists.

In the years after, I took the only trade I could, mother's trade, and learned to sew. I foreswore the sun and the other children, spending time with my crooked back, my careless mother, and my needle.

"Your stoop is fortunate," Mother remarked occasionally. "It allows you to huddle in toward your needle. If only I had your stamina. I wake to a stiff back every daybreak and my stitches come with additional costs." She always then pushed her knuckles into her lower back and arched to stretch her muscles, yawning with an exhausted sigh.

But I never felt fortunate.

Still, I earned a reputation for my work. I never delayed a commission for even a day. And when I was in want of a job, I took garments to the market to sell. There, my work often fetched twice the price of other seamsters. It was said that my stitches held like the chains of Pilate's prisons. City Elders and shopkeepers alike wore my knots upon their backs. To many I was known as the "first needle of Bethlehem," because I kept my word strictly, never raising my price or asking for more time. Though crooked in the back, I was reputed for my craft. That, and the emblem I adorned myself with every morning and every evening—the swaddling forced on me in the streets of my childhood. Each evening I washed it with the rest of my clothes as mother always insisted. And each morning I put it on again. I wore my swaddling to remember the cruelty, and I wore it to remind my mother of her negligence.

More often, the reminder was mine, as I discovered one day while delivering some garments.

"Our child tailor, on time as always," praised my patron, Bartholomew, as I approached. Pointing to my swaddling, he added, "Come swaddled and drenched in the salt of his own sweaty labors, he has." Chuckles issued from faces I could not fully see from my stoop. Several men sat at a breakfast table still couched in morning shade.

Bartholomew traded stock to sojourners and farmers, and butchered animals when their legs grew useless. He occupied the head of the table, and like a king he beckoned me closer. I obeyed, my stance an eternal bow of deference. I placed the package of mended garments on the table beside him and waited for my payment. The man remained mute a moment and made no move for his purse. I felt eyes appraising me: stock traders and animal handlers, whose eyes are accustomed to culling the herd and removing the lame, the undesirable.

Finally, Bartholomew remarked, "You know, Jeremiah, you are not unlike my beasts here. You toil hard, do just as you are told." His insult came in a complimentary tone. For a moment I was unsure how he expected me to respond. So I nodded and said nothing.

Bartholomew nudged the package of clothes. "I respect a man who honors his agreements and delivers on time."

Again I nodded. Inside, I felt a terrible urge to find a wall and cower close to it.

"Jeremiah, will we have your secret today?" my patron asked. He leaned forward in his chair, close enough that I could smell a hint of milk on his sour breath.

I fought the urge to scuttle away, but averted my eyes from his questioning stare. "I don't know what you mean," I managed. "I've no secrets. I am what you see: a tailor with a crooked back and a hump—"

"Like my camels," Bartholomew cut in, pointing to a herd of the animals milling in a pen across the yard. "You see, steady and reliable, just as I said. But you are not honest with me—"

"I am always honest!" I declared. "My price and work are no more or less than what we agree upon." Silence followed my remark. I wanted to take it back. I wanted to collect my money and return to my needle. I wanted to stand straight.

"I mean the swaddling," Bartholomew continued.

"Yes, let's have the truth of it," a man with scabrous ankles interjected. "What makes you wear the garments of a baby? Are you still at your mother's breast?"

Raucous laughter swelled in the morning air.

"I . . . I have them to . . ."

SWADDLING CLOTHES

"I think you'd do better with a traveling blanket across your back and a tether fastened round your neck," another said, imitating the movements of dressing a camel for travel. He returned his hands to the table, his fingernails caked with dark crescents of soil.

Bartholomew watched me the entire time his hirelings cast their insults. He breathed heavily through his mouth, and looked up expectantly from the corners of his eyes.

"I imagine it makes you popular with women, this hump of yours," a third man chortled. "Strong shoulders are a sign of virility, they say."

Mocking laughter spiraled around me. I clutched my swaddling and remembered the cruelty of the children in the street. I remembered mother's ineptitude.

I have kept my word. I have met my half of this covenant. You have your garments on time. This is more than others do.

My fingers started to ache from gripping my emblem so tightly—an emblem of my suffering due to Mother's carelessness.

Raising his hand, Bartholomew silenced the men. In an instant, the animals could again be heard. Birds chirped someplace near. The sudden hush robbed me of my resentment as I swooned, feeling faint. Quietly, Bartholomew said, "I think it is long past time you remove your swaddling, my friend."

I grasped the edge of the table to steady myself. Then I looked directly at my patron. What joke would follow? How quickly would the bright peals of laughter again fill the air? Bartholomew returned my gaze, his hand still held aloft to control his hirelings. I realized he meant his words. His eyes remained firm and held no ridicule. Suddenly, the impetus of a real choice weighed upon my back. I searched Bartholomew's face for help. He said nothing, but gave me time to consider my reply.

The world waited while I reflected on my misfortune and the salvation offered to me by a man with fragrant breath. Without lowering my eyes, I rubbed my thumb and finger together out of habit, feeling the callus created by my needle. Endless hours; a lifetime of huddling over torn robes. Stitching new cloth into wedding garments. Items to make others presentable, beautiful. Clothing for straight backs and square shoulders. And all of it because one silly woman took no time to wrap her child or bathe him with cleansing, salted water. I could hear in my mind the slow burn of my candle from so many night of solitary stitching; it came like low laughter heard from beneath the water's surface, heard across the years.

When I lowered my eyes, unable to do as my patron asked, Bartholomew whispered his regret, "These bands don't seem to have worked in your case . . . you've learned nothing from them."

I touched the straps wrapped around my waist and chest, and offered a faltering smile. I wished with bitter malevolence that Mother could have been with me to see the humiliation she had caused me. I could have turned an accusing finger on her and had ill of her in the mouths of these stinking stable hands. Instead, I half turned, obscuring my view of Bartholomew's eyes and readying my retreat.

Bartholomew uttered a dismal chuckle, then took up the package and removed one of the tunics. He drew the garment close to his face, inspecting the seams. His protuberant nose actually touched the fabric as he evaluated my work. I wondered if he'd know quality if he saw it. Then he pulled at the seams, testing their strength.

He grunted with satisfaction and tossed the remainder of the parcel to the man with scabrous ankles.

"Pass these out," he ordered, "one to each man." Bartholomew swiveled in his chair and regarded me. "Your work is good." Still unwilling to meet his gaze, I nevertheless allowed a smile to touch my face. Compliments were rare, but such simple moments of praise had become my sole reason for picking up my needle. Briefly, I forgot my posture and the swaddling around my waist. The moment was to be very brief indeed. Before I could say "Thank you," Bartholomew derided me: "But you are a fool to sell it so cheaply. Another man would prosper by your needle." His tone became acerbic. "Perhaps you deserve that hump you wear." A look of disgust entered his features and he dismissed me. "Get you gone, cripple, before we cage you with the rest of the animals!" Staring at me, he flung a few shekels into the dirt.

I dropped to my knees to rout the money from the dirt, scraping my nails along rocks and hard earth. Quickly, I scuttled from the table and the private yard, back to my bench and needle.

A few years later the world reclaimed in short order the only two things it had given me: a thief came by night and took all the money I'd saved, and Mother went to her earth. During a short summer night, the purse of coins I kept hidden beneath my sewing box disappeared. No explanation existed but that we'd been robbed. All the next day I sat cursing Yahweh, cursing Mother. I did not pick up my needle. I only twisted my hands into my swaddling and nibbled at the calluses that covered my fingers. Mother kept to herself, and went to bed early.

The next morning, I rose as I always did, and puttered to my chair, preparing to stitch a while before breakfast. The realization of what had happened the day before dawned on me, and I turned aside of my chair and headed for Mother's room, intent on berating her again for the destiny she'd consigned me to. When I knocked at her door, no answer came. After some time, I pushed my way in and found her asleep on her bed.

I called to her again.

No reply.

She appeared peaceful, her body reposed in a restful state. The fret I was used to seeing on her brow had vanished. Perhaps it was always so when she slept. I ventured closer and noticed a bluish hue on her lips. There was no need to do anything more. She had finally left me alone to fend for myself with my crooked back.

With no money to pay for an ossuary, and no intention of placing Mother in a grand tomb, I called for the construction of a coffin. I would find a parcel of ground in the hills, perhaps a cave, to set it in.

The carpenter that came asked for payment before he began his work.

"I had hoped I might offer you work in trade for the building of my mother's coffin." I proposed. "The night before last a thief came to our home and found all our savings."

The carpenter's hopeful expression changed to one of acceptance and emptiness. I might have thought that his own livelihood depended on the sum he hoped to earn for the construction of Mother's box.

"I am well regarded," I continued. "Jeremiah is my name. Have you heard it?"

The carpenter shook his head. "You have no wood from which to fashion the ossuary then?" he asked as if he knew the answer.

"No, but she is a small woman. It shouldn't take much to case her in."

A smirk of irony crossed the carpenter's face. "I have some used shelving wood I can use. Perhaps that will serve well enough."

"I've no concern for the quality of the materials," I sneered. "She did little that warrants my tenderness now—giving birth to me without a father who could provide, neglecting the customs that ensure health and happiness." I gave a dismissive shrug. "Whatever you lay her in is more than adequate. And I'll keep your credit. Just come to me when you have need of my needle."

A tormented look appeared plainly on the carpenter's face. He seemed to consider something for several moments before nodding and taking his leave.

Some of Mother's friends came around to console me, telling me she had found happiness in the arms of Yahweh. I kept my tongue, never telling them that I breathed easier without her around.

Near my lamp I stitched late into the evening,,content with my own company. Often, I looked at the empty seat where she always sewed and mended. Pity clenched my throat. Sometimes I could almost see her there, grimacing against the crick in her back as she concentrated at her work, or stretching up straight and tall as she did when her work was done. I remembered seeing weary eyes and loose skin in her final years.

Then I touched my emblem, fastening my fingers in the swaddling, and glowering at the image of mother that persisted in my eyes. In an instant I dispelled the memories and left her to her earth. Releasing my swaddling, I breathed deeply, retook my needle and my task, bending ever forward into my work.

As the sun went to sleep beyond the western horizon a few evenings later, I finished a job for Michael the innkeeper—several blankets and pillows. I loaded a bag with the items and blew out my lamp. The heat had been oppressive for several weeks, and I found it easier to make deliveries in the evening coolness.

Bethlehem's streets lay quiet. I relaxed and walked slowly, laden with the parcel. My likeness to a pack mule did not escape me. I wondered if I might be nothing more than what Bartholomew had said of me. Since mother died, there'd been no one to talk to, no one to pass time with, no kind word beyond the occasional compliment on my stitching. But the thought of her caused me to instinctively clutch my emblem; a sour taste of bile rising at the back of my throat.

How could she have been so careless with me? I asked myself for the thousandth time.

I hefted my bag higher on my back and rounded a corner toward Michael's inn.

As I came to the entrance, Michael stood conversing with a man whose wife sat astride a mule. The woman appeared heavy with child. Michael was shaking his head, but motioned to the stable and added a few words.

Appearing genuinely grateful, the man led his wife away as Michael noticed me.

"You might have waited until tomorrow, Jeremiah," Michael said. "You've another day yet."

"No advantage in waiting," I replied. I dropped the bag, my back relaxing from its strain. "Would a plate of whatever is hot be worth the day I saved you?"

Michael gave me a reproving look. "So long as you don't make a habit of expecting it. All right. Come in and I'll get you something." He took up the bag with enviable ease, and I went in after him to supper.

I took my meal at a table in the back where food was prepared. By the time I finished, I had learned from an Etrurian vintner that the young couple I'd seen was given quarters in the stable. As I sipped a cup of his wine, I found my thoughts drawn to the expectant parents. Only the very poor would take shelter with the beasts. Circumstances made rough demands of them. Something I understood.

Not long after my first cup of wine, I watched a woman come in through the rear door, a peaceful look on her face. She ignored several questions aimed at her, and went to the fire, where she poured heated water into a large bowl and left without uttering a word.

Still thinking of circumstances and just a little of Mother, I left my second cup of wine and followed the woman. Beneath a bright, starry night, I made my way after her to the stable. I beheld the young mother cradling a newborn son against her bosom as two women mopped her face and tidied a woolen blanket laid over a bed of straw.

I stooped closer, unable to help myself. In the light of a nearby lamp, and in the company of these humble people, I instinctively understood the gift that this new life would be. Mention of a messiah revisited my mind, stories retold again and again by my mother over many nights of hems and knots. I had no way of knowing if this child could be the one of whom she spoke, but the feeling in Mother's voice when she spoke of him . . . the same feeling filled the stable.

I shared a look with the infant's father, then knelt near his mother as the woman I'd followed salted the warm water in the bowl. Suddenly emboldened, I extended my arms without hesitation. "Please," I asked.

With quiet understanding, the woman gently laid her son in my hands. I drew the infant close and wondered if I might have looked like him when I first came into the world. I studied his ruddy features, and breathed in the smell of his new skin. He lay curled in my arms, hardly straight at all.

Carefully, I placed him in the basin, washed him, cleansed him. The vague smell of tears rose from the water, salted as it was. I considered the power of tears to cleanse in both pain and joy. Every cupped hand of salted water I lapped over his soft skin eased the weight of memory I carried. As I administered the simple custom, peace filled my mind and body. And I lingered on the task a moment longer.

When I lifted him out, one of the women handed me some swaddling. I looked at the strips of cloth and felt a great pang of relief deep within me. I smiled at her and shook my head. "No, I have brought my own." With a practiced hand I released the knot and removed what mad been the emblem of my shame and bitterness. How grateful I was that mother had taught me to wash my clothes each day. Quiet laughter of joy escaped me as I bound the child, wrapping him tight.

SWADDLING CLOTHES

Just before I placed the infant back into his mother's arms, I held him close a final time and smiled my thanks. "Child, I like the symbol of these clothes you wear: straightness, honesty, exactness. But these things," I advised the newborn, "come from in here, don't they?" I touched the child's small chest with my calloused fingers. I imagined a response, then nodded and relinquished the babe to the fair woman resting on the straw.

She nestled her son close, and said, "Such a fine first lesson. Thank you." She caressed her baby's face with delicate fingers. Turning soft, intelligent eyes on me, she added, "You walk bent over. It must give you the advantage of knowing the path you tread." She flashed a singularly sweet smile. "If you were any taller, men around you would shrink from your company. Your mother taught you well."

The woman reached for my hand, and I gladly offered it. With the touch, a hundred memories flooded my mind, and at last I had room to cherish them all.

The Rugmaker

I measured the hours in a day by the number of passes I made with my thread through the weave. The days I knew by the progress of each rug. And it was many rugs made in a year, but years before I could fulfill my debt of servitude and earn my freedom. I hadn't the will to calculate the number of passes I must make with my comb before I might walk upon the street a free woman. So I concentrated on each movement individually, listening to the music of my loom as I created something of beauty to dress another woman's house.

There had been days before I arrived at this place and learned the rug-maker's art. But they were a blur, the faces of parents and younger brothers and sisters nearly as blank to me as those of the other women who worked the looms in my master's shop. Four of us toiled beneath the glare of a single, high window. Working there, we wondered what air tasted like on a free tongue, imagined strolling in the street without any particular care.

I didn't blame my family for selling me. Father had lost the use of his back and could no longer work, so they needed the money. As the eldest, I'd helped Mother grow her garden. Together we'd raised the younger ones and tried to make Father comfortable. Confined to his bed, he spoke with the infrequency of a shamed provider, except for the occasional story he told of a healer of men, a great redeemer that would make him whole. I loved Father's stories, but as fanciful and distant as they were imagined, Father never walked a step. So it was mother who transacted the deal that brought me here in exchange for a purse of coins.

While my childhood lay quiet and muddy as the bottom of a lake, the ride to Weaver's Hovel, as we called it, and my first day of learning how to work the loom remained as clear to me as the sky that appeared outside our hovel's window.

Mother put me on my master's pack animal, and I turned in my seat as we rode, waving until the road took us out of sight. My brothers and sisters didn't understood what was happening. Nor, as it turned out, did I. Mother clutched one fist to her breast, holding the bag of silver she'd taken in payment for me, and held her youngest cradled in her other arm. She did not wipe away her tears while I could still see her.

The donkey I rode plodded the road with a lowered head, as though beaten and forever bowing to its life of forced service. With some awe, I noted the country we traveled, occasionally asking questions of the man who led me. He never answered, offering me a dour expression and shaking his head. I'd never been so far from home, and the possibilities of the open road excited me. I began to wonder what lay over each hill, how far the road might go, and what wonders I would have to tell Mother and the others when I returned.

Whatever excitement I'd felt simply traveling the road and wondering about my future paled in comparison to the thrill of seeing my first city. Bethlehem rose from the ground like a mountain as we came toward it. Gradually, the road filled with travelers. Some merchants had set up shop to the sides, and the noise of bargaining carried on the open air with the scent of roasting lamb and the tang of cheap wine. Children scurried underfoot, reminding me of my brothers and sisters dodging and playing near our remote home.

Soon we passed through the city walls. The frantic activity and closeness inside made me queasy. People on errands in every direction, the scent of wood-fires and baking bread, and livestock mixed with the din of the crowds. I felt a smile of amazement part my lips as I clutched at my stomach.

The man who'd purchased me wove through the throng and swilling herds, my donkey obediently following. A few children scampered alongside me, inviting me to play. A few dirty faces looked up imploring me for food or money, until my master drove them away with the switch he used to urge his own mount. Onward we rode, past tall, elegant buildings where men and women finely wrapped in clean garments moved with regal ease through the inner-city streets. Bethlehem swirled around me, loud, terrifying, yet enticing. There seemed a thousand things to see on one street. I could not wait to explore it all. Perhaps the sadness I'd felt a few days before when leaving my home would be swallowed up in a new life of undreamed experiences and bold new tastes and games.

We turned left off the central street and wound through a number of smaller alleys. The sounds of the city faded, a sudden silence overtaking us, unbroken save for the clop of our own animals' hooves.

At a set of doors, the man stopped and looked up and down the alley before knocking at the lintel. A weak voice spoke from within, to which my purchaser growled, "It is Samuel. Now, open up." The door was quickly drawn inward. The man clucked with his tongue and his mule responded, taking him inside. My mount followed.

Inside, the thick smell of newly shorn wool and dyes filled the air. An outer room was littered with straw and plumed with dust. Crates and tattered blankets lay strewn about. A girl slightly older than me stood before us, staring subserviently at the ground. She seemed to await bidding. Samuel slid from his animal and motioned for me to follow. He gave the girl a shove. Together they led me through a small portal into a larger room with four looms, two of which moved and thrummed at the hands of two more girls.

Dispensing with introductions, Samuel pointed for the other girl to take her place at her station, and led me directly to the fourth loom in the far corner beneath the window. I watched from the corner of my eye as the three others picked up a cooperative rhythm in weaving their rugs. I was sure their attention was on me, though they seemed intent on their work.

In that moment I knew the sights and smells of Bethlehem were not for me. The reality of what had happened crashed down on me:

I had been sold by my family, deserted, forsaken. A slave. Suddenly, my heart felt heavier than I knew it could be.

"Here," Samuel said, pivoting on his heel and nodding at the seat before the fourth loom. "You will work here until your debt is repaid. I will let you know when that is. Food will be brought. Your bed is through there." He pointed a short, stubby finger toward another doorway in the far wall. The others can tell you when the day is done." He picked up a lantern and thrust it at me. "No lamplight until it is too dark to see. Those who work evenings will be . . . rewarded." He gave a dubious smile. "Escape will earn you a beating when you are caught. And if you are not caught," he glowered, "I will return to your family and make things hard for them. Don't be deceived about my beneficence in paying for your services. I am hard on those who misuse me."

He stroked his thick beard with his stubby fingers and licked his lips with a short tongue. "Now, the loom is simple. Watch here." He took a flat board wound with a rich, red thread and began to pass it through a series of thick strings with more dexterity than I'd imagined his stubby fingers possessed. Once and back he went very quickly. He then stepped on a foot-lever, which brought a long blade of tines down to pack the thread against the passes already made. "Now you," he said, shoving the instrument into my hands.

Tentatively, I began to mimic what he had done. After but a few strings, I felt the hard crash of a rod over the back of my wrists. "No, no, you foolish girl!" When I looked up into his broad, thick features he snarled, "Don't make me think I've made a bad purchase of you. I've other uses for a young girl that don't offer the comforts you see around you."

I passed a quick eye over the other weavers and a stack of finished rugs piled in the corner. As I did, the man snatched the twine from my hands. "Like this," he said, repeating the weave again. This time I paid close attention, and saw the pattern he made. When asked again to perform the task, I did so without error.

For the next hour, he stood over me, showing me the changing patterns to create the design of the rug. Several more times I felt the sting of his rod on the back of my hands and forearms. When finally he saw I understood, he grunted and shared a look with the girl who'd let us in. I took it to mean that she was to watch my progress.

He lingered at the doorway to the hovel and half-turned to look at me. "Expensive materials, Miriam," he declared, pointing at the wool and dyes. "Do not be wasteful. Each cubit must be accounted for. One rug is worth more than your life." A treacherous smile he gave, pleased with himself. "Work hard. Remember, the more you produce, the faster you satisfy the term of your servitude here and the agreement I hold with your parents. You'll be honest and industrious, or the price you'll pass to others for your treachery and laziness will be high indeed." He dropped the dowel into his palm threateningly. I saw one of the girls flinch. When she looked at me, I saw she wore a patch over one eye.

Samuel left the room with a self-satisfied step. I studied the welts rising on the back of my hands and arms as I went to work. I was unable to find the rhythm of the other girls that day. But I learned the most important lesson of my servitude: in the course of creating a single rug, there were several short strands of twine that had to be cut. With that knowledge, already I began to fashion a plan of escape.

In time, I learned the other girls' names: Bethany, Martha and Esther. Esther was our surrogate mother, and the one who answered to Samuel for what took place in Weaver's Hovel. She had been there for six years already, and still had no idea when she might earn her release. Martha had lost her eye trying to run the second day after she was brought here. Bethany never spoke, though she smiled more than the others.

The man often made surprise visits to check our progress. These inspections led Esther to insist on only quiet talk, no laughter or giggling. We developed a communication through soft words, just audible over the hum of the looms, and an intricacy of smiles that conveyed a hundred differing levels of mirth, like varying volumes of laughter, to measure our delight or joy over something one of us said. Sometimes, when feeling particularly bold, one of us would heave ridicule and distaste, or recall a slanderous joke at Samuel's expense behind his back, all in the set of our lips. Strict training kept those in his view completely stoic. If he'd heard the hilarity and hatred being pronounced so subtly, he'd have taken his dowel to us one and all with great bitterness.

My bed huddled against a far corner in the anteroom. A few things stood on a table for us to tend ourselves, and from time to time new clothes arrived as we outgrew those we came with. We had water to bathe and drink, but we had to ration it closely. Samuel did not believe in waste.

Nights were the hardest. Daytime fleeted away on the strings of our looms, but in our shared room, the awful reality of our lives stared us in the face. There was nothing to do but talk, and it soon became clear that none of us had enough experience in life to keep conversation alive for long. As the years passed, our interaction with strangers was kept to practically nothing, and we rarely met any men beyond Samuel, though the desire to do so flourished as we became women. Most often, we recounted what each of us could remember about life before the looms. Under our second window, cut high in our bedroom, we told of the many wondrous things we'd seen on our short ride through Bethlehem. My recollection being newest and strongest, I spoke last, learning to embellish the details each time to make the moment linger and carry us beyond our prison walls. At such times, voices spoke out of the dark because we dared not risk using oil. Somehow I found simple hope in knowing each of us fixed our eyes on the small square of night sky through the window high on the wall, its far scatter of diamonds gleaming on a velvet black drape.

And when our night talk came to an end, Martha sang in the softest voice anyone could imagine. When we lay still, her bedtime melodies seemed like an assurance of the ultimate end of our suffering. To that sound I fell asleep, myself feeling like a betrayer because of my design to escape, which I could tell no one about. My plan, after many years was nearly ready.

Sun pierced the hovel, shining against the opposite wall in a bright square. As I wove that morning, I watched it descend the wall, preparing to track its daily path across the floor. Before it came to Esther's loom, Samuel arrived with several mules bearing materials. Esther let him in, scurrying back to us with an armload of new blankets for our beds. Panic struck my heart. *He mustn't fuss around my bed.*

I stood, thinking to get to my bed before Samuel could, but he entered and shot me a piercing look before I could leave my loom. I sat down, my hands retaking their task automatically, as I watched him follow Esther into our bedroom.

Those moments became an eternity, and I silently prayed to a God I no longer understood. *Keep him from my bed.*

I heard the scuttle of furniture over the floor and the general tasks of cleaning. Abruptly, they ceased, and though three looms still filled the hovel with work, the silence from our bedroom cloaked us all in a dangerous portent. I fixed my eyes on my work, feeling the trickle of sweat at my temples.

A moment later his voice cut low but clear through the hovel. "Miriam, will you join us? In fact, all of you come in, please." The courtesy uttered in conversational tones bit with impending danger. We obeyed immediately, rising from our looms and filing toward our bedroom, forced to pass beneath Samuel's arm, propped across the doorway.

Once we were all in, he paced casually, hands clasped behind his back as though conducting a military inspection. He licked his lips above a mountainous beard and assumed a friendly gaze as he passed before us. Never had I seen the man behave so; my heart pounded in my ears. Martha raised a hand to shield her good eye each time Samuel passed her. The reflexive act of preservation told me much about what was about to happen.

"You girls have a good life," Samuel began. "Oh, I know, you'd like to get out more."

, I scoffed privately at that. We never got outside.

"But the streets are no place for young women," he went on. "You are safe here, which is more than most young flowers can say."

He touched Martha's cheek gently as he invoked the soft image. I thought it callous and deliberate of him to do it, knowing her fear for her eyesight. "You have food," he boomed, anger edging his voice now. "You have beds and blankets. You have the blessing of learning a trade and skill that will serve you when you have earned your freedom."

Again a doleful internal mirth blossomed in my breast. None of us believed we would ever be free of him. I believed he knew as much.

"After all this, and the generous gift of compensation I made to your starving families to elevate your lives as I have, I am repaid with treachery and betrayal." He whirled and looked across us with a palpable disdain. His eyes showed clearly his estimation of us as yet another asset, one more difficult to maintain because of our need of food and water.

He went to the corner and stood before my bed. I knew then that he had found me out. I felt the urge in my legs to run. The door would be open from his arrival. I could beat him there, his belly fat from the prosperity we supplied him from our looms. Maybe I could reach home ahead of him, warn my family. But did I remember the way? And what if they no longer lived where I had been born?

Even as I found his poison gaze resting on me, I thought to run and flee anywhere but home. Anywhere but to the family that had sold me into bondage. Let them suffer for their sin! I remembered Father telling me the story of the many-colored coat. But no Joseph would I be to their starvation. Let them have restored to them the measure of their vile deed. I could feel heat flush in my neck and cheeks. I returned Samuel's harsh look and felt my last bit of hope—

hope of finding and forgiving my family, hope of escape—hanging tenuously by a weakened thread.

With a savage hand, the man lifted up my bed, revealing a hollow beneath filled with pieces of twine in an array of colors. A thousands snips or more of rug materials, clipped and stowed for the purpose of fashioning a rug of my own, a final weave upon my loom that I had intended to carry into Bethlehem and sell to purchase my freedom. He had said it himself the very day he confined me to this hovel: "One rug is worth more than your life."

Holding my eyes fast in his awful stare, he knelt and thrust a hand into the pile of thread. He took a fistful and held it toward me. "A thief have I bought! A thief have I fed and clothed and protected!" He looked at Esther. "Will you tell me that you knew nothing of this?"

She remained mute.

The man stood and raised the fist still holding the privily stowed clips of my freedom. Esther waited for the blow to descend, but the man did not strike her.

"No, I believe you did not know." I watched the logic play over his face. "You would not have endangered your friend's good eye, nor the child Bethany could not care for when her husband died before she came to work for me. And you certainly would not have put at risk your own nearing release." He lowered his hand, casting the bits of thread back into the shallow hole beneath my bed. "I think Miriam acted alone. A willful girl, an unappreciative girl."

He strolled toward me, allowing his large presence to diminish each girl he passed until he stood before me. "What foolishness," he snarled. His breath smelled of onions and garlic. Standing so close I could see the kernels of grime that had taken root in his large, open pores. "No doubt you thought to weave your own rug, to sell it on the market for money to buy your freedom." He laughed, taking hold of his ponderous belly. "Did you consider the quality of your weave with the many knots your thread would contain from tying so many scraps together? Did you consider what trader would take you seriously on an open market, a girl with one pitiful rug to sell? Did you consider how quickly I might have found you? What about the honor of the contract made by your parents?" He leaned close. "It is not my fault they did not want you."

The insult washed over me in a plume of moist, stinking breath. His short tongue ran a film of saliva over his cracked lips. "I have papers, Miriam, your papers. And you should not underestimate my influence on the city streets. The signatures of many men and women rest upon my books, contracts for favors I've yet to claim. The life of a waif without a home is nothing to them that owe me. Take care . . ."

A broad smile returned to his face, parting his lips to reveal yellowed teeth. His bulbous nose spread with the merriment, and he let out a guttural chuckle. Promptly, he returned to the hollow beneath my bed. He motioned to Esther, who took an armload of my trove and bustled away. Next Martha, then Bethany, both bearing away much of the slow accumulation of my dream of freedom, leaving only a handful of short thread. He bent and lifted these himself, stuffing the threads into his belt pouch.

He strode from the room, pausing in front of me long enough to say, "I wonder how your roommates will feel about this? How wonderful a thing is friendship, toiling together, living together, no doubt dreaming of freedom together. Yet your idiot plan did not include these friends of yours." A smug smile spread on his thick features. With astonishing speed, he drove a large fist into my belly. When I doubled over, he grasped my hair and hauled me upright. Bits of my thread fell from his fingers onto my forehead and nose. Samuel blew the pieces off my face with musky breath, the smile never leaving his face. He then let go of my hair and left the room.

When I regained my breath, I went to my hole and peered into the emptiness. Years of silent hope. Years of securing away the smallest lengths of twine and thread. Too many rugs to count, too many days of pilfering only what could be cautiously cut and stowed away. All of it gone. It felt like a lifetime of careful secrets and patient accumulation was lost in the briefest moment. I wanted to curl up in the hollow and lower the bed. I could not face the years it would take to rebuild the stash of thread that I had just lost. And even that had not been enough to make my rug. "Nearing release," he'd said. But I knew he had no intention of ever seeing me free. No more did I even have the anger or energy to take flight in the streets and test my chances there against my captor's influence. I wanted only to lie in the dirt and forget that my family had abandoned me, forget my puny plans for my own rug, the looms, and simply breathe the scent of dry earth and focus aimlessly at the dark beneath my bed.

Instead I lowered my bed and returned to my loom.

The others were not angry with me. That night as we spoke, staring up at our window toward heaven, Martha, Bethany and Esther marveled at my courage and determination, asking questions about how I'd kept my plan so secret all these years. When had I started, and when had I expected to start my rug? We spoke most of the night. Before we were finished I'd decided to start again. Somewhere beyond that window lay a life for me without fear and bondage. I wouldn't abandon it now. I told the others of my desire to begin again, and at once they all offered to help. Between us we created new hiding places, several of them. Each girl began adding their own snippets to my cause. For their help they asked only more stories of me, inviting me to tell them of what I'd do when I broke free, where I'd go, even the food I'd eat. The stories became an endless dream about my life liberated from the hovel. We kept that flame burning in our hearts from the simple tales I wove with my words in the small hours of the night.

How many rugs we wove in the years that followed I couldn't guess. We showed more subservience than before in our jailer's presence, which is just what he expected. We'd all become women. Though we still feared the smite of his dowel, our fear changed from that of simple physical punishment to one of inviting his suspicions. At night our talk turned to thoughts about the possibility of rearing our own families, and whether our time had passed us by for such a miracle. Youth no longer sat upon our brows as dew-like as when we'd first come to Weaver's Hovel.

My pile of short threads grew. One night while we looked up at our window in the dark, I began to fasten them together into one long weaver's thread. Each night I worked at it. Soon, I had a spool and felt a spark of hope in my belly at the prospect of walking on the street beyond our hovel's walls.

Not long after, I was ready to begin, and sat at my loom as darkness descended. I worked as fast as I could, weaving through the latest hours of evening without pause. When full dark came, I wove my rug by memory, without light, my hands finding their regular patterns. The sound of my loom seemed large in the silence, and I feared it might give me away, but on I worked without stopping.

Day broke and I continued. Having chosen to gamble on his confidence in our subservience, I prayed fortune would smile on me and Samuel would not come that day. All that day I worked, the others checking my progress and feeding me bites of food and tipping a cup of water to my lips, because I would not stop. My fingers ached more painfully than ever I remembered, but still I would not slacken my pace.

Fortune did not smile, nor did she frown.

As light fell in russet hues from our window, Samuel burst through the door, spitting insults and irritability. Rarely did he bring someone with him to Weaver's Hovel, and those he did always wore the same menacing grin when they surveyed us. This time, the man following Samuel paid us no attention, imploring our jailer for his own sake.

"I need just enough to begin," the man pleaded. "It isn't much, Samuel. I can repay you when I'm given the work to complete."

Samuel laughed derisively. "If you are good enough to earn the work, why are you currently broke?" He brushed past the man and gathered a few carpets into his arms.

"Times are hard," the man supplied. "Carpenters everywhere suffer just the same."

"Indeed, and where would I be if I began lending money to craftsmen who can scarcely afford to eat on the merits of their trade."

Samuel dropped one of the carpets in favor of another. "You should have considered the possibilities before your wife became pregnant."

Martha gasped. Esther shot her a reproving look. But the carpenter had Samuel so flustered that he hadn't noticed.

"Perhaps you are right, but that is the past and I can't change it." Of a sudden, the man noticed the rest of us sitting at our looms. His eyes brightened. "Perhaps I can be of service to you on your looms. Are any of them in need of repair? I will trade the labor for money."

Samuel whirled. "This is none of your concern, Luke!" he blared, pointing savagely at us.

Now more aware of us, Samuel's anger completely preoccupied him. It was not likely he'd notice that the rug I wove was my own.

"Of course not, but what I ask is paltry." The carpenter showed open palms. "I wouldn't come to you if it wasn't necessary. No one else has money to lend." He paused. "And I must think of my unborn child."

Waving his arm at us, Samuel said, "I've my own children to think about. Enough! Go! You'll have no money from me, and you've taken too much of my time already."

A moment longer the carpenter entreated Samuel silently. Our jailer returned a baleful stare. Quietly, Luke stepped from the room and closed the door on his way out.

The looms never stopped humming. Samuel cast a quick look across us, his cheeks red, his breath labored. Trembling from his own frustration, he yelled, "Not a word!" Then, he picked up one more rug and left the hovel.

A series of expressions passed rapidly between us, lengthy conversations conducted without a sound. My stomach roiled at the thought that Samuel would not lend money to a man willing to repay it. Could he then ever be trusted to free us? What punishment would he inflict on me if I were caught with my rug trying to escape? I left the answers to themselves and concentrated on my weave.

When night fell again, I went on by rote, familiar with every knot, every string. Soon, even the sound of the loom came like a distant drone. I felt removed from myself by fatigue and the endless weave of my knotted thread.

By morning of the second day, my rug was complete. I pulled it from my loom and wrapped it tightly, stowing it in a remote area of the entry chamber behind some empty casks. I fought sleep that day, and managed to work until dusk, when I could stagger to my bed.

For two days I rested, working at a relaxed pace, regaining my strength and natural sleep rhythms. On the night of the second day I awoke to the sound of excited voices. As I opened my eyes, I beheld a star like a beacon shining through our bedroom window.

"Never have I seen that one," Martha gasped.

"It *is* a beautiful star," Bethany said.

We all looked at her, silently amazed at the sound of her unfamiliar voice. None of us commented. Bethany speaking seemed appropriate just then.

In the great light of the amazing star, Esther turned to me. "I think it is a sign, Miriam." For a moment I wasn't sure if she meant the star, or Bethany breaking her silence. "Your rug is ready. It is time for you to take your chance. There is no better time than under the cover of a blessed night. You'll assure yourself of being first at the market when trade begins tomorrow."

I looked around at my friends, whose faces were pale but

hopeful in the soft light of that bright star. They had become my family, and I had brightened their lives with nothing more than the wanderings of my imagination when night came. I wanted to speak, tell one last story, but could only stand and hug each woman close before preparing to go. I retrieved my rug and slung it over my back with a woven cord. Then, working together, we created a human ladder under our bedroom window. Esther stood against the wall, Bethany climbed onto her shoulders and carefully stood, then Martha helped me balance as I climbed to Bethany's shoulders. My hands barely reached the window ledge. Using all my strength, I pulled myself up. I paused on the sill to look back at my friends. I waved, regretting that they could not come with me. Steeling myself, I dropped from the window to a nearby roof, and crossed to an alley behind the Hovel. Slowly, I lowered myself as far as I was able, then let go and fell a free woman into the Bethlehem streets.

Painful though my parting was, sweet was the breath of free air I took as I left Weaver's Hovel. The alleys and byways stood mostly empty, and I strolled down their centers discovering a wide panoply of stars and the quarters of families and businesses even I might never have dreamed of in the stories I told the others. The joy of taking steps in a direction I did not know, toward something I could not see, filled my eyes with tears of joy. With my rug tucked under my arm, I sensed a weight lifted from my chest and chains released from my legs. I began to run, to test my own strength and feel the burn of rapid breaths in my throat. I gloried in every feeling and exhaustion. Freed from my cage, I began to laugh. I panted and loped through the darkened city, redeemed by the snips of thread woven and tucked beneath my arm.

Faster I ran, sweat coursing freely down my skin, away from a bag of coins exchanged for my life, away from the looms and the stale air filled with the scent of old wool and barren, earthen floors. My legs burned, but I gloried in the sensation.

Soon, I slowed, tired but happy. I passed a crowd gathered near a stable. Commerce usually took place during the day, but perhaps in this mob I might find a merchant ready to have a rug at a good price, good enough to emancipate me once and for all.

I came upon the people huddled together and slipped between them, keeping watch for the hawkish eyes of a man of business, eyes like Samuel's. None could be found. Those assembled in the mouth of the stable showed meekness so obviously that I despaired of finding a buyer.

When I came through the twist of men, women and children, I found myself standing in front of a child laid in a manger. His parents sat beside him. How poor must they be to have birthed the child here? Soiled clothes they wore on their backs, and around them the musk of the stable clung to the very walls. Still, none of it seemed to burden them. They looked at me with soft eyes and smiled. I suppose it was the look I might hold if ever I am blessed with a child of my own.

At my feet I noticed a number of items laid near the manger, some of them broken beyond repair, others just ordinary items, the presents of a poor class. I winced as I thought of the poverty of my own parents, so dire it had driven them to sell me into bondage. I looked deep into the father's eyes as he gazed upon his babe, and up from my childhood came the story my father had often told me of the messiah. Sometimes he'd embellished the tale, adding things he couldn't possibly have known. Other times he'd spoken the story simply. But always it caused a rash of chills on my skin to think that one man might come into the world to save an entire people. I smiled to think that perhaps I had learned my knack for telling my own stories from my father as he lay an invalid upon his bed, and that his injury was the reason I had been sold to Weaver's Hovel in the first place.

I followed the father's eyes to his son. As I beheld the child, a flash of memories careened behind my eyes: silent laughter shared with my weaver friends, a donkey ride into Bethlehem. The removal of my first pile of thread, a dowel rapped across my wrists, and my mother not wiping her tears away as she watched me disappear down the road of my childhood. Looking on the babe, a flush swept over my skin, a thrill and peace all in one. At once, I felt eternal hope as this child and his parents bore indignity with such grace and honor. I knew it then as surely as ever I've known anything: this was my father's messiah. The rise of the hair on my arms and neck told me as surely as the peace I felt inside.

Again I became aware of the gifts at my feet. What ransom might be paid with these items? That's when it came to me. Slowly I knelt and inclined over the babe. "Stories of you softened the harshness of my childhood . . ." Emotion choked my words. I waited for my voice to come again. "Since then I have told many tales, but have forgotten the grandest story of all." I peered into the infant's small eyes, my own eyes damp again with a sweet sadness and lingering joy. "I will not forget again."

I wiped my tears away. "You have redeemed me more surely than my rug could have, child. More surely by far." I shut my eyes, and so as not to disturb the reverence around me, I smiled the subtle smile of the Weaver's Hovel. If they could only have heard the great joyful sounds that smile conveyed! Then, sharing a look with the babe's mother, I said, "That you might never be parted from each other." With that I placed my rug at the foot of the manger, knowing its value would serve them well.

I stood, still smiling as loudly as ever, and took myself back to the streets of Bethlehem, unencumbered by my rug. I was free. I knew it. I might go anywhere in the world and carry the feeling with me.

I ran, faster than ever I had, feeling brisk air rush into my lungs, and straining every muscle within me. Beneath the light of the great star I moved with all the haste I could muster back to the hovel, to my friends, to my family. Tonight, and every night, if only to lift and ease them in the days until their service came to an end, I would tell them the grandest story one could ever tell.

The Watchman

With the army of Tiberius, I headed into the highlands of Urartu. All the while I felt the eyes of my comrades on me, wondering what valor the grandson of Crassus would display in war, the grandson of the man who put down Spartacus. Rome expanded daily, and my assignment here came by special request. The Armenians claimed a Providence that chafed the Emperor's sensibilities about divinity, and had defied the Emperor in allying with Parthia. Augustus would be watching his stepson, Tiberius, and his men closely in the highlands of Urartu. A man might build a reputation with such attention.

Dusk fell, revealing a broad spray of stars across the night that seemed only slightly more numerous than the countless cook-fires dotting the expansive fields below. An arid cold pressed in, causing our men to huddle toward the flames. Excitement attended conversations, the thrill of immanent battle prickling my skin as much as the cold.

"Rumor has it these beasts bleed a lineage that flows from a distinguished line," Marcus said, his mouth hooking into a satiric smile. He only ever spoke to incite argument.

"Yes," answered Titus. The eldest amongst us, he'd marched three campaigns, returned to Rome for legal training, and come again into the frontiers, marching two more campaigns since. Placing a hand over his breast in mock deference, he announced, "They go back a hundred generations to a prophet named Noah, who sailed the only ship upon a worldwide sea that drowned the entire family of man." Titus dropped his arm and laughed over a mug of mulled wine. Pointing to each of us with a deliberate finger, he said, "The men of brass and spear is what we are. Don't forget that. The glory of Rome tempers every edge we swing and hardens every shield we carry. Is it not so, Lucius?" He threw me a confident look.

I drew a knife and tossed it up, catching it safely after two complete revolutions. "I've no regard for the legends of barbarians. The wheels of progress belong to the Emperor, and they churn the unyielding beneath their rightful path!"

A wave of applause and cheers erupted from the men around me.

"You've a commander's tongue," Marcus baited me, "but it is one thing to spit the name of Mars when smiting a savage." He paused to pick a shard of meat from between his teeth. "It is something else to wage war against an enemy who dies as readily for his god as we do for the glory of Rome. Men of brass and spear create new Roman borders with might and the brilliant tactics of Tiberius." He tossed the piece of meat into the fire. "But the Armenians lead charmed lives. Ask any forward scout."

Those gathered around the fire waited for my response. They all knew what reputation was mine to fill. I could best any man with a sword and the strength of my arms, but I would never lead if my words did not inflict the same decisive punishment, demand the same respect.

I stood, delicately placing the tip of my finger to the point of my knife's blade. "It sounds to me that you've no metal in you, Marcus. The taste of blood is that of inflexible copper, yet may drip from you as soft and sweet as honey." I lifted my blade to my mouth and slid my tongue across the flat, metal edge of the knife. "This is the taste that fills my tongue. This is the instrument of my honor."

I stared at Marcus. "Do you have the metal that Crassus had, to crucify an army at the roadside of the Appian Way? This is the metal that must exist in every man of Rome. Look into the faces of those who die, and know you are justified in all you do as an emissary of our homeland.

"These we challenge tomorrow in battle are no different than the last, or those to follow. More men of brass and spear may die in this campaign than have died in previous battles. But a future war will surely send a greater host of Roman sons to their graves . . . It matters not." I inclined my face over the fire that it might catch the full light of the flames, and lend it a sinister mien. "What matters is the heart that beats within you! Is it Roman? If so, then it beats with a thousand other hearts, a thousand times a thousand! Against it no lineage may stand, however noble or divine it claims to be." I sheathed my blade with aplomb. "Few men have chosen to contest with the strength in my arms. It is wise of them, for these hands are bent toward the glory of Rome, and against such no one is safe."

The clatter of blades beating against breastplates rose fiercely into the night with the embers of our fire. Before I could accept their praise, a collective howl shattered the night, drowning the applause. The Armenians had come under cover of darkness! Soldiers quickly leapt to their assignments. Likewise, I dashed to untether my horse from a siege catapult.

Deadly arrows whistled closely past us in the night. Our bowstrings hummed in response, blindly flinging arrows back into the darkness. Torches lit and bobbed as men rushed to meet the foe cascading toward us. A baleful glow from the collective flames rose up and touched hundreds of faces, glinted off scores of blades.

My horse reared as a flaming arrow sliced past his nose. I clung to his reins, trying to calm him, but soon lost my grip. When the animal dashed away, I turned to help maneuver the catapult into position to hurl its armaments. In a long line beside us, others did the same; some already unleashing large boulders high against the cloak of night. Distantly, the crash of the giant stones into crowds of men was heard.

Eager to play my part, I pushed my shoulder into the work, and lost my footing. I tumbled to the ground, unable to stop my fall. The momentum of the wheels carried the catapult onward. Before I could roll to safety, the large machine crushed me under its great weight.

For an instant, the cries and blaze of battle filled my senses. Blood rushed in my ears, like the heartbeat of my own pain. Then my sight blackened as unconsciousness claimed me . . .

Days later, I awoke in a hospice not far from the shores of Lake Van. Tiberius had moved east with the army, driving the insurgent Armenians ahead of him. He would quell the barbarians, but would do so without me. I stared in horror at my bandaged legs, swollen to twice their normal size. At that moment I did not consider that I would never walk again. I only thought of the missed opportunity to stand upon the field of combat, giving honor to my grandfather's name.

When the swelling receded and the pain had diminished, I was left as a great sack of flax, able only to move by pulling myself across the floor with my arms. Weeks passed, and my vain attempts to walk did little more than acquaint me with the hard reality of falling repeatedly to the ground. A hundred times my legs collapsed beneath me before I realized with despair that my military career was over. When I ceased trying to stand, I bitterly resigned myself to the only vocation left to me—a beggar on the streets of the kindest city I could hope to find. I might have returned home to Rome, but to what reception? A crippled and useless grandchild to my great progenitor, Crassus, perhaps to lie on a bed and be catered to because my name and not my deeds merited it?

No.

I did not return to Rome. My ignominy remained mine alone. For a time, I stayed at the hospice. My legs healed, though they remained unusable. My spirit languished without remedy.

I did not eat much. By force of will, I took some wheat broth when my stomach ached from hunger. But soon, I suppressed even this. I sat with my back to cool stone and stared for hours into the dimness of the inner corridors of the hospice. At times, wails of pain rose from rooms at far corners of the place, and often moans seeped up from the floor below. We were a collection of misery; a mob united in human suffering. The smell of convalescence hung thick in the air like the smell of mildew, like so many exhaled breaths uncleared by the new breeze of an open window. Into the miasma I gave a sad offering from my own lungs; an old song my mother had used to lull me to sleep. With an untrained voice I quietly lulled my own grief.

Weeks passed and I became emaciated. Touching my cheeks, I could feel the hollows beneath the hoary beard which sprouted riotously on my face. I didn't care. The grooming so conspicuous among the ranks meant nothing there. I believed that place a living grave, and found a kind of peace in the feel of its fallow dirt beneath my hands, and the ripe stench of straw too long used as a bed. What honor I had brought to the name I wore? Grateful that none knew my family, I kept my name secret from all, though to my memory it remained a painful reminder of my past.

One day, a woman with diseased skin scuttled timidly toward me. Red splotches and white ulcers stole up her arms and beneath her chin. Her hair hung clumped and matted around bits of straw and twigs, fused in a dirty tangle. The gamey woman wore the pallor of one who had been at the hospice much longer than I. The thin blanket wrapped around her bore stains, the source of which I dared not know.

Yet for all of this, clarity shone in her eyes, the smallest tinge of hope, as though her condition were temporary. I marveled at the look, vacillating on whether it were hope or lunacy.

"You must eat," she ordered, appraising my wasting frame. "The broth is not enough to sustain you."

"Leave me be." I rolled away, barbs of hay pricking the skin on my arms.

"You've lost your legs haven't you?" A bony finger jabbed my thigh.

I whipped over, bringing my face close to hers. "I haven't lost my arms, and my dignity no longer prevents me from striking a woman. So be gone! Eat my portion if that is your desire. I've no care to digest charity rationed on grimy plates."

"The pride of Rome lives in your diminished breast," she chided. "It won't be long before you'll choose between that and your very breath."

I thought to reprove her with stinging words about the smell she bore, her lack of beauty, and the demise she surely faced as her disease bubbled her pale skin. Seeing these things, preparing my barbs as I had done around the cook-fires of a Roman battalion, I was suddenly humbled to think that a conquered nation's poorest and most ailing denizen would concern herself with my health. The light in her eyes, and the jut of her collarbones beneath her skin, softened my heart. I realized then that she spoke earnestly, not from self-gain. With a weak hand I patted her misshapen fingers.

"A little pride I have left, my lady," I smiled faintly. "But it strengthens me only as much as the measly broth. You are right, of course. I should eat. But I've lost the strength to drag myself to the meal line, and nothing is left when they make rounds to feed the rest. I'm afraid the wheat broth will have to do."

Her lips curled into a splendid smile, despite the wattled skin around her chin. The smallest gesture of touching her ailing hands seemed to enliven her. "Nonsense," she declared. "I'll bring you some. I've developed quite the skill in crawling along the floors to supplicate for my supper." A charming wink followed. "I'll bring you some bread and a piece of meat. You'll believe yourself back at your Roman table."

Before I could answer, she crawled away. Even among the hospice workers, I had never seen such eagerness to serve another. And from one whose own strength must surely have small limits, whose life's time marched to a rapid end! I wondered what advantage lay for her in doing me this favor. Did she expect something in return? Yet, even as she disappeared around a stone wall, I knew it wasn't so. It might simply have been that looking her own death in the face had taught her a truth I hadn't seen.

Distantly, I heard the mulling of feet and snippets of conversation over the food lines. It came as a quiet murmur, much like the lap of waves upon the shores of Van. In response, voices deeper in the hospice cried out in anticipation of their own supper. On the air, the scent of wheat and boiled meat wafted, mingling with the smells of the unwashed and the implacable stone and earth and shadow.

The sound of hurried movement approached me. Gradually, the pace of footfalls and labored breath echoed ahead as someone rushed to where I lay. Around the wall came the woman, scrabbling with all her might to stay ahead of two men who clawed and raked at her back. She yelped as a wounded cur, scurrying to get away.

THE WATCHMAN

One man grabbed her makeshift dress, and ripped the blanket away, exposing her skin to the languid light of the inner confines of the hospice. She labored forward, determined. The fabric gone, I saw she clutched food to her breast, and instantly knew the object of the men's desire. The one who'd pulled off her garment shrieked and thrust the blanket away, renewing his pursuit of the food she carried.

The other leapt, diving on her back and pushing her to the ground. They tussled mere paces from me, the man fighting to snatch the morsels of meat and bread from her hands. With all her strength she fought him off and made a few crawling strides toward me. The second man hunkered down, pulling at her arms to halt her progress.

Without mercy they ripped at her thin limbs, trying to win the food from her clutches. Outraged, I growled deep in my throat, wanting to rise to her aid. I pushed myself away from the wall, but stabbing pains immediately shot behind my eyes and into my head. My vision greyed, and I collapsed back, cracking my skull against the stone. I leaned over, hoping I could drag myself to her defense with my arms, those same arms that had served me well in Tiberius' army, and had made men tremble at the thought of personal contest with me. But one effort to pull myself forward over my straw brought my shoulders low, my wasted muscles unable to support me.

With supreme frustration, I screamed at the woman's attackers, but was ignored for my impotence. I watched the woman fight to keep hold of the food she had retrieved for me. She cried, the pain of her struggle no doubt intensified by the disease rippling her skin. The men did not relent, and soon her strength waned. They succeeded in yanking free their prize. Rough laughter echoed off the walls through mouthfuls of food. Ridicule and triumph accompanied the new smell of meat and bread.

"Foolish woman," the first man sneered, "to claim good food for yourself, when your life is almost over."

The second man followed the woman's pained gaze. "Or did you bring these treats to the Roman dog? For that you both ought to be killed." He laughed. "But we'll eat your ration and that will destroy you sure enough." He stepped on her back, injuring her further as he walked away.

The other man followed, eating noisily to punctuate his triumph with added insult. The woman's eyes now shone with tears, her body still convulsing from the fight.

I wanted to hold her, console her, to thank her because what mattered was her desire to help me, not the food that had been lost. But I could not move, my power and prowess were gone. Not only from my legs, but also from the arms I'd boasted all my days as a man of brass and spear. I had not been able to stand in defense of a woman whose errand had been to aid another in need of sustenance . . . In my shame, I was glad of the deep shadows, the cold, fallow earth, and the oppressive smell of decay. They suited my darkest hour, when the grandchild of Crassus had suffered a kindness to go undefended. The stinging barbs of straw upon my cheek as I lay witness to the woman lying naked, trembling, and unchampioned were my only punishment. They did not hurt me near enough.

I ate thereafter, to regain the use of my arms. Shamed, I could not bear to stay at the hospice after the woman died. Her name had been Helen.

I had not married, and my parents had long since passed this life. So, there was no reason to grieve about not returning to Rome.

My humiliation prevented it in any case. The grandson of Crassus, a clumsy fool who slipped beneath the wheels of a petrobolos. The distance between what I'd meant to accomplish with my life and where I'd fallen to, made the very thought of Rome tormenting. Perhaps it was pride or self-pity, but I could not go home again.

My only friends were in Tiberius' army, and they were not men to rely upon beyond the battlefield. I had no place to go, and no idea of how to survive the wiles of the gods. Many were the times I railed against Jupiter and Mars for leaving me in such a condition: a derelict without the spirit to do more than beg for alms. But my cries fell on deaf ears, as I scuttled along the ground to filch scraps of discarded food and usable rubbish. Over time, that was how I arrived at Bethlehem.

I spent years in remote byways, watching the progress of age in my face as reflected from pools of rainwater. The thick whiskers growing unruly from my hollow cheeks had taken over my face. The scorch of sun and blight of wind hardened my skin to leather, markings of the street. At night I curled up on those same streets where by day I cried for alms.

At times, I thought I might put to use some of the skills I had learned as a soldier in the army of Rome, performing some menial task somewhere. But I could never bring myself to do it. Any useful thing I did reminded me of the station I'd aspired to, the name I'd never honor. Such thoughts stole my confidence, my dignity. I think I peered into the rain pools because I needed to remember that I was alive.

Seated near one such puddle, formed this time from a leaky water trough, I asked passersby for mercy in the form of food. A determined looking man moved past me, his shadow gliding over my pool and obscuring briefly my own reflection. He noticed me in passing, neither smiling graciously nor frowning with contempt. Preoccupied, he continued on, and I watched him vanish in the swarm of humanity.

Perhaps an hour later, the man came again from the other direction. I spied him early, and noted his progress toward me and my puddle. Deep inside me exasperation and rage began to mount. A hundred people, two hundred, passed me daily and said nary a word, offered not a single coin. But this man, crossing my way twice, inspired wrath I had not felt in years. I would have something from him.

It may have been that I saw in his eyes, in his purposeful gait, the image of the man I'd set out to be. That he could walk at all brought new resentment, which burned behind my eyes.

Closer he came, his eyes fixed ahead of him, oblivious to me. I did not raise my hand for an offering, but sat with my shoulders squared to him, my head upturned.

As he came within a stride, I could see a blend of disappointment and ire seated on his brow. With his next pace, he stepped into my looking-pool, splashing me and muddying the water.

Before I knew what I was doing, I lurched forward and wrapped my arms around his legs. I fastened to him with all the strength I possessed. The man crashed to the ground, grunting as he hit. He immediately twisted onto his back and began to thrash his legs. I hugged them tightly, but one foot got free. Then he nearly kicked the other loose, but I took hold with my arms and determined that in this contest I would hold on or die trying.

"What are you doing?" he blared.

"I won't be ignored!" I spat. "I may be low, but I am not inconsequential! You showed me your indifference not once, but twice. Then you stepped into my puddle and soiled me."

From his expression, he surely thought me mad. "I stepped in your what?" A quick glance at the rippling water in my pool brought understanding to his face, then renewed concern. "Let go of me, or I'll have you jailed."

"And where is the threat in that?" I countered. "Do you suppose they'll feed me, give me a dry bed? I should have taken you down when first you passed, and spared myself an hour's indignity on the street."

The man ceased his struggle. He breathed heavily for a moment, when a smile curled on his thin lips, turning soon to laughter. He dropped from his elbows to his back and laughed from the pit of his stomach, lifting hearty cackles to the slice of sky I watched at night.

He made no attempt at trickery, no move to scoot away. And the sound of his joviality coaxed laughter from my leathered face. Soon, we both lay on the street near my puddle laughing loudly toward heaven. A few passersby gawked at us, but neither he or I seemed to care.

When the moment passed, he propped himself up again on his elbows. "I've nothing to offer you," he said through diminishing smiles. "If I did, you'd get double what I usually give for the brief detour you gave me from the misery of my life."

"The misery of *your* life?" I mocked.

The laughter began anew. Through the amusement he managed, "The irony is that I was on my way back from trying to beg money from a miserly moneylender." Between blurts and blasts he said, "He turned me down, too!"

Finally, the laughter abated and he looked down at my arms, still fastened to his leg. "You've got powerful arms, my friend. Certainly not the arms of a beggar."

I released my grip. "Yes, but that is what I am." I sat up and noted the mud in the puddle settling to the bottom again.

The man sat up, too. "Well I'll make you this promise, my powerful friend: I am on an errand to secure materials for a job, one that is proving most difficult. But should I come to an agreement for this contract, I'll seek you here to offer you a job."

Stunned, I could say nothing.

The man stood, chuckling warmly. "My name is Luke," he said, offering me his hand.

I took it. "I am Lucius," I replied.

His grip was strong. And though towering above me, he looked me in the eye in a way I'd not been regarded in a long time. I held a small reservation about whether he'd make good on his word, but it felt good to acknowledge another man in such a way again.

Then he let go and went his way.

The next few nights passed without the man returning. In the darkness I watched the sky, gazing at the glimmering points of distant light. From my bed of spent cloth and discarded robes, I lifted my eyes to my slice of heaven beyond the high walls of the forgotten alleyway in which I made my home. It was there that I found some sense of peace, and a vivid awareness of how much shorter I stood without the height of my legs beneath me.

Sometimes it grew cold. On such nights I sang my mother's lullaby for comfort. It always sounded lonely echoing off the walls of the narrow corridor, where I remained hidden from the scowls of weary night travelers and drunks. But even a lonely song has power to encourage another day of life.

It was on such a night that I saw the great star in my slice of the sky. I was nestled into my sackcloth when I realized the light above me was not the moon. I lay back and watched with amazement at the unequaled brilliance of the solitary heavenly body. How like me that star was, I thought: solitary, distant . . . important. The thought surprised me. Somewhere beneath my ragged clothing, I still wanted to live, still believed I held some special significance. Or perhaps it was only that poverty had made a philosopher of me.

Soon, repeated footfalls dashed past the entrance to my alley heading east. It was far too late for any sanctioned gathering to be taking place, so I knew that something significant was happening. I had learned that it was always wise to be on the periphery of any large crowd, where the act of charity to a beggar without legs would be duplicated by people of conscience. I dragged myself from my bed and began to pull myself along behind a solemn woman who walked with purpose.

Through the quiet city I crawled, my legs scraping the ground. Others passed me, heading in the same direction. Quiet excitement filled the air. I kept on, and soon came to where the people gathered: a stable for the keeping of livestock at one of the more affable, but meager inns at this quarter of the city. Many of the attendants were not merely shepherds and laborers, but tradesmen as well, and a few in rabbinical robes and Roman political dress. The mixture puzzled me, but I thought it might prove lucrative, should the wealthy be inclined to stoop toward me with their purses. I drew close to them. As soon as I had done so, I felt suddenly very pathetic and wretched to be feeding on their sympathies in such a way. Something vitally urgent undoubtedly had brought them to this place in the stillness of the night, and here I sat, the former heir to Roman military glory, with an opportunist's hand prepared to petition them.

Shamed, I began to turn away, hoping to steal unnoticed back through Bethlehem to my bed, when I heard the most splendid sound. It was the innocent cry of a child new to this world. A child born in a stable. Looking up, I noted again the great star, and imagined that it shone for this child, right over his bed, like mine. I imagined that perhaps he was like me: alone, cold, maybe these people had come to offer him alms, so poor and wretched was he.

With that thought, I pulled myself through the crowd, around legs, through the refuse of the livery and beds of the swine. I needed to see this child! What manner of birth was this, that in the stinking hole of a stable resided a babe so adored that the people of Bethlehem would come to pay him homage in the coldness of the night?

Men and women parted as I neared the lamplight, skulking forward across the straw toward a lovely young woman and a sturdy fellow who looked proud but tired. They both stood like stewards at the side of a feed-box. Set upon short legs, the makeshift bed was too high for me to see the child's face. Cautiously, I drew closer.

I spared another look at the child's parents. Their faces expressed an invitation to come closer still and see their babe. Dragging my lame body beside the wooden crib, I stuffed my useless legs beneath me to give me added height. I took hold of the box's side and propped myself up, resting my eyes upon the infant who had made the sound I had heard out in the night.

I stared at the child for a long while. I knew he was not cold, he was not alone, and he was not wretched.

I knew then, that I was not alone, either. Nor was I wretched.

I put forth my hand and rested my dirty fingers on the swaddling clothes. I so wished that I had something to give him, to thank him for making me to feel tall without my legs. I gazed with adoration at the wondrous child, then looked again at his father, who seemed ready to fall from exhaustion.

"Sir," I said, "You are tired and can hardly sit up. I was once a soldier in the army of Caesar and brave as the lion. I am grandson to Crassus the Lean, and a mighty man of brass and spear. Do not let my legs mislead you. I am yet strong in my arms, and I will watch this child so that you might sleep."

The man opened his mouth as if to contend with me, then closed his lips without a sound. He nodded solemnly toward the babe. "Thank you, my friend. Watch well."

He retired to a spread of straw near the back wall, and I smiled at the woman across the manger. I then put my arms upon the crib and wrapped my hands tight against its side.

And that is how I stood guard one last time. Stood without my legs, and watched over the baby whom some of the crowd were calling a king. It was my finest moment, and I found honor again in my bosom, even as my grandfather had, and more. For my new king's only requirement was the willingness of my heart. I have never stood taller, or served more nobly than on that night. I was not a beggar. I was not wretched. I was he who watched this special babe on the evening of the great star, holding his cradle fast in the recesses of the night.

The One

I sat with tired hands on a low rock, dusk blurring the vividness of trees in the distance. Slowly, I massaged my fingers and palms, trying to rub some of the roughness out of them. It was no use. Some of the scars had been there since my bar mitzvah. Examining my hands, I could see where the ravages of the sun and wind had cracked lines in my skin so that the delicate patterns in my palms were no longer discernable. My knuckles had become the smooth white scar tissue of healed scabs. But I had never lost one of my herd, I thought, as I sat upon my low rock and considered the past. Ah, but that was not completely true, was it . . . The memory threatened to surface, but I quickly shook it away and cast my gaze out upon the flock, which milled quietly as light fled the sky.

Night birds began to stir, alerting one another with distant calls. The fragrant smell of olive groves floated on gentle breezes as I picked up my crook and ran my hand along its smoothness, thinking of its maker.

Under the glare of the sun a few days past, I had happened upon a man sitting beneath a cypress tree.

"Taking refuge from the heat?" I inquired, stepping into the shade myself.

"I'm afraid it isn't any cooler," he replied. "But it saves me from the sting of sun on my skin."

"I'm Ishmael," I introduced. "Humble shepherd and handy with a sling." I tapped the strap hanging from my belt.

"Luke," he responded in a weary voice. "Poor carpenter in need of wood." He lifted a cypress branch and shook it.

"Seems a hot day for gathering wood," I observed.

Luke nodded. "And I forgot to bring water." He eyed the water-skin slung over my shoulder.

On the other side of the tree rested a handcart, several branches and pieces of wood piled inside. From where I stood, I surveyed the contents closely. At least one of the branches would suit a proposition I decided to make to the carpenter.

"Well, Luke, I suggest a trade."

He gave me an understanding look. "And what do I have that interests you?"

THE ONE

I strode past him and took up a long, hooked branch from his handcart. Wheeling back to face him, I held it out. "You're welcome to as much water as you can drink, if you'll fashion me a new crook."

"Done." He reached for the water, which I gladly gave him. Once he'd refreshed himself, he wiped his mouth with the sleeve of his tunic and took the branch I'd picked up. "What happened to your old crook?"

"Broken. I was separating a few of the stubborn sheep and it cracked."

He nodded, then drew a knife and set to tooling the wood into a serviceable shepherd's staff.

"What need is strong enough to bring you out on a day like this to scour the hills for wood?"

Without slowing, the carpenter said sourly, "Foolishness." He carved a few moments longer and stopped. "Actually, it is the hope of fulfilling a promise."

Casting my eyes up the hill, I recalled standing with my papa on a precipice and talking of promises before he died. Not wanting to cry for no apparent reason in front of a stranger, I suppressed the memory, instead attending to the skill of the carpenter's knife.

Before long, he handed back to me a smooth, well-honed crook. I thanked him, and without any great ceremony, he stood, lifted the handles of his handcart, and pushed out into the blazing sun.

Thoughtfully placing the crook aside, I withdrew my sling and small pouch of stones, the latter culled from a nearby stream. Putting a rock in the thickened length of hide, I swung it around my head to test its weight. Then I sent the stone sailing into the darkening night toward a tree that stood silhouetted against the dusk.

"One . . two . . three," I counted, before a loud whack echoed into the shallow vale beneath me. Pleased that I was still deft with my sling, I praised myself mildly before returning the weapon to my side and resuming my vigil at the edge of the herd.

Waiting for full dark to descend, I nibbled at a piece of cheese and counted the sheep, which had begun to settle down to sleep. I surveyed the surrounding area, attempting to determine the ways a predator might try to approach the herd. The hill I had chosen for a vantage point overlooked the entire valley, and at the base of a large sheer rock I lay unharrowed by winds. It was a good place to hole up for the night. From here, I could see the entire flock. Casting a stone downhill was much easier than trying to sling one uphill. Still, the predator was not responsible for the death of a sheep; as Papa had taught me: *The reason sheep die is a poor shepherd.* The memory of that lesson never left me. As I recounted papa's words, the memory I'd tried to forget resurfaced in savage detail. In an instant, I could see Sarah, the one sheep I had lost and been unable to save.

One day when I was a mere boy, Papa had gone into the city to trade for food and a new blanket for my bed. His absence necessitated my first sole supervision of the flock. After a long set of instructions, he gave me a firm handshake, just like men do, and told me to protect the sheep. I remember how my heart filled with joy at the opportunity to justify his faith in me.

After he left, the skies grew black. Hours passed. Rain began to pelt the land and thunder rolled out of the hills to the north. The storm beat down on the herd and tore at the night. The loud boom of thunder pushed the air as it exploded around me. Lightning streaked earthward, frightening my sheep and threatening to scatter them.

Quickly, I drove my animals into a small rock alcove at the edge of a meadow. The sheep grew more skittish with every lowering crack of light and the loud rush of air as peals of thunder ripped around us. I worked back and forth across the alcove to keep the herd contained. With each step the mud oozed between my toes and pulled at my feet. The air became thick with the smell of damp wool. I wiped my eyes free of the rain, and used my crook to settle and position the frightened animals. I took a count, calling specifically to those few I'd named. The routine always calmed me when I fretted for their safety. Yelling to compete with the storm, I lifted my voice over the patter of hard rain on the ground.

"Joel, Michael, Sarah, Ezra, Esther, Jumpy, Noisy . . ."

Sarah was missing.

My heart sank. Papa would be back soon. I thought quickly. The escarpment that rose at the end of the meadow held a cave. If I could secure the sheep there, I could try to find Sarah before he returned. I called for the sheep to move. Trying to hurry, I slipped in the mud and fell, taking a mouthful of muck. Screaming, I rose and spat out the foulness. It took some work, but I eventually herded the sheep to the cave and cajoled them into the darkened opening. They would not likely wander if I raised some kind of blockade. Casting my eyes through the rain, I spied some low brush. With my knife, I cut several limbs from nearby trees and bushes and stacked them at the entrance with some large rocks to secure them. Then, I took my crook and ran out into the storm.

I retraced my steps, but soon my own footprints had been washed away. Into the night and rain I called out for Sarah, often unable to hear my own voice as thunder rolled over me and washed my words away. Soon, I began to run blindly in the dark. I squinted against the drops hammering my face and tried to watch my footing as I searched for Sarah.

Through dense thickets I ran, the limbs scraping my legs and scratching my arms and cheeks. My skin already cold from the freezing rain, stung the more at the insult of whipping branches. I became disoriented, searching for a landmark to fix my location. Nothing looked familiar. As I pressed on, I lost my concentration, and my foot caught on something. I dropped again, this time into a field of rocks that bit deep to the bone. In that instant, I thought I knew what it must feel like to be struck by a rock thrown from a sling. Lying there, with the smell of wet stone and mud all around me, the desire to give up tempted me. But as the pain abated, so too did the will to give up.

I realized that if I failed, Papa would lose trust in me, and I might never inherit a flock of my own—his memory was long and unrelenting. I dropped my face to the ground and wished for the rain to cover me over, sweep me away. Face down in the mud, I remembered a hundred days of mild sun and wind, green meadows, and gentle instruction from Papa as we surveyed the sheep. Listening to him, I had felt his love for the animals. In time he had imbued the feeling in me. I knew that if I never found Sarah, Papa would be disappointed. Then, with my nose caked with wet earth and grass, I realized he would not be the only one: I wasn't sure if I could ever forgive myself.

After lying there for several long moments, I lifted my head toward a stand of low brush. There, caught in the thick branches I saw a few pieces of bloody wool. "Oh, Lord, no!"

I jumped up and scrambled ahead. Removing the wool from the stiff branch, I shielded my eyes from the storm and peered over the low growth. Just beyond it, a ravine cut away and out of sight. I rushed through the bushes, taking no care for my legs, and raced headlong down into the ravine. The wind howled, driving the rain as a thousand thorny pricks into my skin. Flashes of lightning painted everything in bright relief for brief moments before the blanket of night fell in again like a pall. I shuffled my feet to keep my balance, pin-wheeling my arms as I slid and jumped and ran toward the bottom. Another bright flash from the sky showed the uneven ground clearly, but when darkness reclaimed the night, I lost my footing a third time. I tumbled and rolled down the embankment, my crook jabbing me in the chest before twisting out of my hand. When I came to rest, I lay a moment, heaving, staring up into the sky this time, the rain still pounding down upon me.

When yet another stroke of lightning lit the world, I saw close to my outstretched arm the limp body of my dear Sarah. The sight was awful and messy. Predators had ravaged the poor creature. Little remained. In the rain, I wept. First for the life of the innocent lamb, then for myself because I had failed. The storm continued, and I sat in the mud praying that Sarah might have her life back, yet knowing it would never be. Deep inside, part of me resisted the grief for a single lamb, and resented even more that I had grown to place so much importance on such a thing. Soon, I seemed to cry only to cry, unsure what the tears were for, only glad the rain washed them utterly away.

Hours later, still sitting there, footfalls sounded through the rain. Up the ravine I saw my papa staring down in anger and disappointment. His face, highlighted by the streaks of fiery light, was sharp and his eyes were changed toward me. I wondered if he regretted that I had experienced such a loss without him there to comfort me, to explain things as he so often did. But when he left me there with the dead animal, I decided his feelings were not so sympathetic.

I think part of me sits there still.

Papa did leave me the herd for an inheritance. I was his only child, and though I never regained his trust, I never lost a second sheep. All this, of course, came at a cost. I never married. It seemed that a man who devotes so much of his time to a pack of beasts was not a powerful candidate for the hand of a woman. Nor did the smell invite many to tarry too close. And though I possessed a clever tongue, I rarely had the opportunity to see or speak with the fair creatures of Bethlehem, because the herd was often restless. Perhaps, though, all these were merely the excuses of a weak man, because there was a woman once, a woman I met one morning at a well.

We shared many such mornings walking together and talking after her water was drawn. There seemed nothing we could not say to one another. She had the gift to draw things on paper, beautiful things. And I told her about the herd, and the things Papa had taught me. I believed I loved her. But after it all, I learned of *one* thing she had not been able to tell me. I learned her to be a woman of low reputation. Before I ever spoke my feelings to her aloud, I stopped going to the well.

Still, I had the satisfaction of being a good steward of the flock. I was a vigilant guardian, and despite losing Sarah, and that one woman, I learned to love being a shepherd.

My memories receded, leaving me sitting upon my rock with scarred hands. Night came on full, and I began to take my last count of the herd, pausing at each sheep to fix the animals' places in my head as papa had taught me to do. Nearly finished with my count, I realized Shaky was missing. Shaky was a yearling whose legs had never seemed to firm up properly. He always looked ready to collapse. As I stood to make a closer inspection of the herd and see if Shaky were truly gone, I heard voices from the top of the hill. Turning, I saw two young shepherds careening down toward me. They shouted to me, and I thought perhaps they had found Shaky dead or injured. My heart pounded.

"What is it?" I called up the hill.

"Come, Ishmael! Come, quickly! We must go yonder to Bethlehem!"

It was Caleb, a good shepherd, but too fat to get around to protect his herd as he should.

"What are you saying, Caleb? Slow down."

"Samuel and I have seen an angel over on the hill of good grazing. He announced the birth of the Messiah, come to a virgin bearing the babe in a manger in Bethlehem. We are going to find this child. Come with us! Hurry!"

"It is true," Samuel added.

"Have you been at the bottles of Julius the vintner, Caleb?" I reproved.

"Nay, we have a sign. The child shall be wrapped in swaddling clothes, lying in a manger. Even now, the Savior of this people is among us, born this very night! Come this moment!" He waved his arm frantically, giving me an urgent, earnest look.

In my heart, a warm feeling spread as I scrutinized the expressions on Caleb and Samuel's face.

It was true!

I had heard the prophecies myself, the words of King David. It now seemed our deliverer had come, as it had been promised.

Caleb pointed heavenward. "Look there, Ishmael, it is our compass." I followed his hand and saw a star, set deep and bright in the evening sky. As I looked at it I felt my chest resonate as though the star were a sure testimony, a witness of the words Caleb spoke. Of the words papa had once spoken.

The memory rose in my mind as it had beneath the cypress tree days ago. This time I let it come . . .

Not long after Sarah had been killed, papa led me to a promontory overlooking the valley where the herd fed. In silence we climbed, dusk filling the horizon with crimson color. From the place where we stopped, hills and terrain stretched as if forever, touching the sky at infinite points. Winds licked at our cloaks, stirring the hair on my brow and drying my eyes. I stood beside Papa, waiting for him to speak. Few words had we shared since the death of Sarah.

Finally, Papa ended the silence. "Ishmael, a day will come when things will change for us. A mighty, wonderful day. Do you know what I mean?"

"No," I said, wishing I had a better answer.

"This," Papa answered, sweeping broadly with his arm toward the view we shared, "all this, belongs to Yahweh. He created it for us, asks us to tend it mindfully. To watch and learn . . . and grow."

"I sometimes hear the others speak of deliverance," I offered.

Papa hunkered down beside me, still facing forward toward the sunset. "Yes, Ishmael. This is the day we live for." He raised his hands and touched thoughtfully the scars that marred them. A vague smile came to his lips. "But this day, this deliverance, Ishmael, it is not something that will happen without our assistance, our agreement. It simply isn't possible. It isn't the way of Yahweh to compel us down a certain path." I thought I heard emotion thicken in Papa's voice, as though his words held a second meaning. It was as if he spoke of me and the path *I* was on, of his own efforts to direct *my* path.

"He doesn't," I answered, hoping Papa would hear the forgiveness I intended—I kept my crook now because I wanted it, not because Papa wanted me to follow him.

Papa put one of his arms around my waist, and I knew he understood. My heart loosened then, the few words we'd shared relieving the tightness and discomfort between us.

Papa went on. "We must partner with Him, Ishmael. We must begin this process that is likely to take all our lives, to mature, learn wisdom . . . learn forgiveness."

I nodded and put my small arm on Papa's back.

Another smile tugged at his wind-dried lips, furrows of burnished skin folding at the corners of his eyes. "You are well begun, son. Perhaps so am I. Shepherds are we. Minding the flock, caring for the young and feeble, leading them to deep grass, sleeping with a crook in hand should trouble come, a sling to defend the herd." He squeezed my waist. "It is a process, Ishmael, a climb worth making. The One that comes to deliver us will show us the best path to its summit. But there is work to reach it."

Again I nodded, happy to feel his comforting arm around me.

"But when at last we come to our goal," Papa said wistfully, "what a view we'll have."

"Agreed," I said. And we shared the rest of that sunset reconciled, in silence.

"Let us go," insisted Samuel, interrupting the memory.

The image faded from my mind. I smiled gratefully, ready to accompany them, when the sound of a bleating sheep reminded me of my last count. Looking over my shoulder, I surveyed the flock. Shaky was still nowhere to be seen.

Caleb and Samuel began to climb, as if assuming I would follow.

I lowered my head and said a prayerful apology to the great God of Heaven. Then I said to my friends in a small voice, "I cannot come with you."

Caleb wheeled about. "What?" he blurted, a fevered incredulity clear in his voice.

"I have a missing sheep. I must find him before he comes to harm."

"Are you deaf and dumb?" Samuel followed.

"You are mad!" Caleb yelled, his features puffy and stern. "Ishmael, this is the greatest moment of our lives. You should rather lose *all* your sheep, than choose not to come this instant!"

I stood unmoving, unable to understand what I had done to deserve a moment as this, such a choice. Yet after all the words and desires were gone, there was no choice "Go on with you. I must find my sheep. I will come if I can." I waived a hand to dismiss them, and heard them grumble as they climbed toward the city. Their parting left me to a bitter loneliness I never remember feeling in all my life. And still, upon the tapestry of my mind, the only image I could see was the look on my papa's rain-soaked face as I lay near the one I'd lost.

THE ONE

After placing all my wood on the fire to ward against the predators of the night, I took my sling and crook and set out. My prayer this time was dual: to preserve Shaky, and to preserve myself, for I had denied my King to save a beast.

I ran into the darkness, clutching my sling in my right fist and swinging my staff rhythmically with each long stride I made. I retraced the way we had come, the flock and I. By the light of the very star that might have taken me to the Deliverer I chose my steps that evening, running and peering into the darkness.

On I raced. Against the terrain around me, awash in the glow of the star above, I sensed a stormy night from my childhood. I thought I could smell mud and wet grass. My legs tired, my eyes blurred with the sting of sweat, like rain in my eyes. Aloud I called for Shaky, and heard an inner voice echo a cry for Sarah. I jumped over outcroppings, tumbling through stands of low brush. I felt more the lashing of switches from the memory that unfolded with surreal similarity, than the reality around me.

Then, just as I had done that fateful night years ago, I tripped and sprawled on the ground, my nose filling with the close scent of earth and resignation. I lay there, praying again, hoping when I rose this time I did not fall to the side of another lost sheep.

A thought occurred to me. Maybe if I didn't stand up, this time there be no rain soaked smell, no father to come indict me. Perhaps if I just slept where I had fallen and let all else pass away . . .

Then, a second thought: had I really forsaken the opportunity of paying homage to the Deliverer my papa taught me about in order to seek one missing lamb?

I laughed bitterly and inhaled a mouthful of dust.

145

Suddenly, from the darkness came a mewling. I rose quickly and followed the sound. Over a knoll I sprinted to a shallow river we forded early in the day. Standing mired in the mud on the other side, Shaky bleated helplessly. In the bright light of the great star his body trembled, and I immediately saw why—not ten feet from him was a snarling wolf, poised to descend and make a meal of Shaky. My hand began to quiver. I could see nothing but papa's face and Sarah's torn and bloody body. I would never make it across the river in time, and the fear in Shaky's throat seared my heart. I spared a look toward the star and wondered if this might not be my punishment for betraying the sign and not going to the babe.

Shaky bleated again feebly, losing strength. The wolf began to creep forward. I looked at my worn hands and remembered the same scars covering Papa's fingers and palms. In the similarity, I found confidence. Slowly, I took a large stone from my pouch and placed it in my sling. Narrowing my gaze across the river, I swung the rock about my head, gauging its heft and the distance I must throw. When my sling began to whistle, I let go of the cord, and the rock flew out across the water, across the night sky and beneath the star. It sailed past Shaky and hit the wolf in the chest, bowling it over. When the creature regained its feet, it scurried into the night. Shakey stared after it, still bleating weakly.

I meant to rush across the river and retrieve my sheep, but my feelings overpowered me and I fell to my knees. "I have not let them have the sheep, Papa," I whispered. "I kept my flock whole." I laughed and cried, the sound of it lost in the current's flow.

When my strength returned, I waded the river and hooked Shaky with my new crook. The animal cowered close to me, suddenly quiet.

Taking the lamb up in my arms, I offered thanks for the fulfillment of promises.

Several days later, as I sat at my evening fire, I again heard footsteps approaching from the darkness as I had the night Caleb and Ishmael had come bearing news. I was not far from the city, so I expected to see any manner of persons traveling along the path. I stood to greet the strangers and saw a man and woman coming toward me.

They paused upon the road and hailed me. "We seek Ishmael."

"I am he," I replied. "Who are you?"

"May we come to your fire?" asked the man.

"Yea, draw close and warm yourselves." I sat again, taking a quick inventory of my sheep. Shaky was there.

The couple came and sat round my fire. As the woman came within the glow of firelight, I thought for a moment that my one former love from the well had sought me out, so strikingly did this woman resemble her. But this fair lady held a small child in her arms and cooed maternally to the babe. I soon realized who they were. I knelt on the ground and bowed before them.

"Please, come closer," the woman said.

I raised my eyes and did as she bade me. When I was at her feet, she put her hand out and laid it tenderly against my cheek. I regret that I recoiled at her first touch. Not because she was not fair and kind, but because the touch of a woman was so foreign to me.

"I am Mary. This is my son, Jeshua," she said, looking down upon the babe in her arms.

The man knelt beside us. "I am Joseph, Ishmael. We have been told that you did not come to Bethlehem to see Jeshua because one of your sheep was lost."

"Yes, it is true. I beg your forgiveness. It was foolish—"

"Ishmael," the man interrupted, "your faithfulness to your flock is no less than the reason this child comes to the world. That you tend it with such steadfast loyalty, leaving the many to save the one . . . it is a pure, noble quality. May Eternal Father bless you for it."

I listened to the man's words, while his wife nodded. As I looked upon the child I somehow felt he also agreed.

"Now tell me this," Mary said with a knowing look. "I might have thought you knew me when I first sat at your fire. Have we met?"

"No, dear lady. It is just that you look very much like a woman I once knew."

A mysterious smile brightened her face. "What happened to this woman? Was she your wife?"

"No," I repeated. "I learned . . . our union was not meant to be."

"Could she draw?" Mary asked plainly.

I returned a disbelieving stare. My mouth hung open, and I dropped my crook. "Yes," I muttered.

Mary fixed me with an intent look. "This, too, is the reason for my son's life. And the woman you mention is changed." A smile returned to her lips. "I thought perhaps you'd like to know."

Joseph smiled, as well. I drew closer and touched the cheek of the Deliverer my Papa had spoken of on the mount not far away. Behind me, Shaky bleated for attention. And it was not lost to me that these good people and their child king had journeyed into the night, away from their home and hearth, to visit me and ease my burden, one lone shepherd.

The Beggar

When I lifted my palm and lowered my eyes before the traveler arriving at Bethlehem, I watched his feet. Much may be learned about someone from the care they take of their feet, and the sandals they wear. Of course, I still wanted him to place a shekel in my outstretched hand, but I did not expect it. And I had never taken such interest in the sole of another until my husband Mark died beneath the assault of an angry mob's stones, not until I lost my home and came to Beggar's Row to make my petition on the charity of travelers at the gate.

I was one of many mendicants lined up in the shade of the outer wall. I had even less a chance of receiving alms because my face bore scars from those same stones that claimed my husband's life. Even among beggars, prejudice favored the handsome or beautiful. It was yet another reason to hold my head low when generous passersby reached for their purses. As often happened, the traveler's coin passed my upraised hand and fell into the fingers of the woman kneeling beside me. I heard her whisper, "God bless you," as she stowed the money away.

The heat of the day penetrated our slim strip of shade. I kept my shawl forward over my head, hoping for success with other taxpayers coming to the city to report. In the lull between travelers, I took the sack from beneath my skirt and removed the last pair of sandals—all that remained to me of my husband, Mark, other than memories. He'd been a sandal maker. Since his death, I had been reduced to selling the last of his stock in order to survive. Now I removed the final pair from the bag. They were his finest work.

Touching them, feeling the careful stitching, I imagined I could feel Mark's hands performing their delicate work, crafting a comely item as well as one durable and worth much at market. The smell of the leather reminded me of past evenings after supper, when we had sat close and talked while he worked the materials into their proper form. The smell of lamp oil and well-used tools accompanied us. Content, I had smiled often just sharing his company.

Selling what was left of Mark's work had fed me when I could beg no supper money; the sandals fetched me decent exchange. But though my belly grumbled, I had delayed parting with the last precious pair. Perhaps I feared I might forget Mark once they were gone. And I wanted to remember—remember what he stood for, and most especially the valor he had shown in maintaining the integrity of his own beliefs and witness, even unto death. Holding that last pair to my nose I remembered.

During one of our evening conversations, Mark looked across the table at me, pausing in his work.

"I have been praying about the messiah, Rachael," he said. "Praying and reading. And I've had a feeling begin in me. It grows stronger each day." He held up the sandal he worked on to study it closely. "It grows stronger as I tool each strap, each sole. And not just a feeling but an image, as well" he enthused, his eyes dancing in the light of our lamp. "I see the feet of the Matchless One who will walk this land to bring us new hope, new freedoms. It is a fine pair of feet, Rachael, very fine." He caught me with a rapturous stare. "Do you know what's remarkable?" he asked, not waiting for a response. "That in my mind they are the feet of a servant, a meek man who walks great distances to sit in the presence of the sick, and mourn." He paused, then added in a voice grown husky with reverence and love, "Mourn with those who suffer, touching them with tender hands, healing hands."

"Is this the one Yahweh will send to deliver us from the Romans?" I asked. "Such a man would be a blessing to anyone, but how can he change the course of things with meekness?"

Mark smiled and bade me come to him. He stood and gently sat me in his chair. Then he fetched a basin of water and brought some cloth and oil. Kneeling before me, he patted his knees, urging me to rest my feet on his legs. Tenderly, he removed my sandals and began to wash my feet. With loving care he cleansed my skin, looking up into my eyes, the same smile playing upon his lips.

"You're showing me how this man will turn our hearts," I said.

Mark's smile widened, but he did not speak. I relaxed at the massaging motion of his hands anointing my feet with oil. His firm but gentle touch soothed me, and the soft scent of olives hung fragrant in the air. I closed my eyes, losing myself in the humble service Mark showed me.

When he finished, he waited for me to open my eyes before speaking. "Rachael, I don't know if the Matchless One will have feet as large as yours," he laughed mildly, teasing as he often did over the size of my feet. "But I have a feeling he'll be every bit as kind as you."

"And will you comment on the oddities of his feet as well?" I pushed gently with my feet to rebuke him.

Mark gave his easy laugh again. "I suppose I might." Then, his smile faded, his eyes growing distant, as if seeing far beyond the walls around us. "I do hope I live to meet the man who uses those feet. I do hope to offer him something to ease the footsteps of his journeys." He rocked forward and folded me into his embrace. A moment later he set again to his work, perhaps thinking that its wearer might be the very man of whom we'd spoken.

As I watched him in the quiet repose of our modest home, I knew Mark was right. A leader would come to relieve our burdens, but he would do so with the patience of a long walk, and not the quick arc of a sword or spear. My husband had been blessed with a humble knowledge. It forever shaped the care he used in the production of something as simple as a sandal.

Not long after Mark had first shared with me his impressions about the coming of our messiah, someone came pounding on our door. It was still early, and our two children, Lezra and Naomi, played in the corner in their bedclothes. Mark rose from the table to answer. The moment he opened the door, rough hands yanked him into the street. I rushed to the doorway to see what had happened, and found myself hauled savagely outside and cast upon the ground beside my husband. I struggled to my knees and turned toward the door, where my children stood watching us with wide eyes through the legs of several strangers.

"You spread lies and heresy," one man called, kicking dirt into Mark's face. "It is spoken on the street and in the homes of devout men that you claim revelation about the messiah, and that he comes as a submissive dog to lap at the feet of our occupiers." A general grumble rose in agreement.

"I say only what I feel in my heart," Mark replied. "My soul finds peace in the thought of—"

"Silence!" the man commanded.

I looked up and saw Simon, who sat chief among the Pharisees at temple. He glowered down at us with such malice that I feared what these zealots had come to do.

With narrowed eyes, the rabbi began in a low voice. "Your soul is clearly inhabited by something unclean, Mark Bar-solof. Your words corrupt our most sacred beliefs and hopes." His lip curled back from his teeth as he said, "One might think you take payment from the Romans to spread such seditious slander! What more could Rome want than a Messiah who cowers beneath her evil hand? I've thought more than once that you do too well for yourself, making only pitiful sandals. Could it be that your children are nourished by milk drawn at the teat of Roman swine?" Simon sneered, and again a consensus sounded in guttural grunts.

Mark looked over at me then, a vague half-smile hid from the mob by his shoulder and arms. He meant it as comfort, and, I've thought since, as a parting farewell. Raising his head, he showed calm eyes to Simon. "I have taken nothing from Rome. I desire deliverance as much as any of you here." His eyes shifted, and I saw surprise registered there. I followed my husband's gaze to see Silas standing in the crowd. In that instant I knew this dearest friend had spoken of Mark's intimate impressions of our future savior. His words had brought this judgement upon us through the chain of rumor-mongers who do nothing more than eat and talk, growing fat on their meals and arrogance. A sheepish look crossed Silas' face, and he shrunk from view. "But I have sensed that he comes to teach compassion," Mark continued. "That he might be recognized upon our streets, in our synagogues, and at our lintels," Mark spared a look to the doorway, where our children wept quietly, "by the quality of kindness and forbearance such as we ought to show our children."

The insult was not lost on Simon, who refused to look at our traumatized young ones. The Pharisee replied, "And will he not correct our foolishness as we ought to correct our babes? Will he let mercy rob justice? Yahweh's law is absolute, Mark, and not something that can be compromised, even by the messiah. Strict governance in the home brings children out of their childish ways, and into the light of Yahweh's law. Something which you must now satisfy."

"No!" I cried, and struggled to stand. Something struck me in the back, driving me to my knees.

My children cried out in protest. Instinctively, I scrambled toward them. Several bodies attempted to block me, but I surged around them and raced toward Lezra and Naomi. As I reached and embraced them, a man wrapped his fists in my children's clothes and wrestled them from my arms. Shrieking with panic, Lezra and Naomi grabbed for my legs. I fought against the man until a booming voice silenced the crowd and ceased our struggle.

"Your children are not safe in your care," Simon declared. "Left to yourselves, look what invidiousness has plagued you. You place at naught the dictates of the holy prophets, of Moses who led us from the bondage of Pharaoh. Your children may be the seeds of noxious weeds in a fruitful garden." His words crept over me like the terrifying images of a nightmare in the first moments before it stirs the dreamer awake. I felt their meaning though I could not name it. Then, he made it clear. "We can either draw them by the roots and place them in fertile soil, or rake them aside with the burrs that prick and clutter our harvest."

I looked into the upturned faces of my children, who were clinging to my legs.

A silence stretched in the street before our home. "Quickly," Simon ordered.

The man began to pull Lezra away again, but the boy fought him. Naomi shivered against my thigh. Without thinking, I beat at the man's wrists to unfasten his grip. Squeals of fright vibrated against my leg, muffled as my daughter buried her face from the world. The moment seemed endless, and I spoke forceful prayers in my mind, making offerings of myself if Eternal Father would only hear my pleas.

As if in response, Mark spoke from where he still knelt upon the ground. "Rachael." It was all he needed to say. With gentle firmness, I broke Lezra's grip; the man whisked him away in an instant. Then, I knelt before Naomi and prepared to speak to her. Before I had uttered a word, a second man pulled her away. The terror in her eyes also stole her voice. In a moment, Naomi disappeared from sight.

Grief wracked me. I could not hold a single thought, as raw emotions tore through my body. Anger swelling and yielding to hatred, hatred yielding to sorrow, and sorrow to helplessness. Finally, numbness cloaked my senses, and without knowing how I got there, I suddenly found myself beside Mark again.

From the crowd an unfamiliar voice shouted, "Can the man deserve such treatment for mere impressions and words? What of his wife, his children? Must they share such scorn?"

I followed the voice to a man standing on the flank of the crowd. Deep furrows rippled around his eyes as he looked on at what was happening.

Simon silenced any further comments with but a glance. The look intimated that sympathizers could meet a similar fate.

Drawing the Pharisee's attention back, Mark said, "You may exact your punishments, but I cannot recant what I have said." He gave Simon a forgiving look. "And if you'll search your own heart, you'll feel what I have felt."

Simon hunkered down before us, his prayer shawl bunching around his waist. His lips pursed between his whiskers as he framed his words. "It is deception that convinces you to oppose the wisdom of your spiritual stewards, Mark. And you have led your wife down to destruction beside you. I will pray that the mercy you hope for finds you." Simon lifted a stone from the street. "But it shall not rescue you from the bite of inflexible rock. Even in this rock we are instructed as to the nature of Yahweh's will and decree." He turned the stone over in his palm. "Firm . . . more enduring than the flesh of mortal bodies."

Mark showed his accuser forgiving eyes, a look I feared because I thought I also saw resignation in it. "But never so everlasting as the spirit, Simon, which outlasts stone and seeks Yahweh even in the face of certain death."

Simon shot a hateful look at Mark, then at me. Brusquely, he stood and waved angrily at us. The crowd herded us up against the wall of our home, and soon, like a fall of rain, stones and rocks flew at us with frightening speed. Some stung a moment only, others hit heavily. They felt as though they bruised the very bones within me. We huddled together, Mark trying to shield me as much as he could. The aim of our assailants came expertly, and the hail continued unabated from every direction for what seemed an eternity.

Mark placed his arms over my head and turned his back to the mob. Too quickly, his arms around my shoulders loosened, and a weak groan escaped his lips. He slumped back against the wall, and I lost consciousness. I don't know how long I lay there, but when I opened my eyes, the street was as quiet as a graveyard, abandoned by even the normal pedestrian traffic. Mark lay dead beside me. A new loneliness like I had never known came over me in that silence.

The crowd that stoned us had assumed me dead, and would return soon to carry our bodies away once we'd been sufficiently seen as an example of heresy. I could not lift one of my arms, but with the other I managed to drag myself into the house and close the door. I was alive, but my death felt as complete as if I'd never awoken. Everything had been torn from me—my husband, my children . . . my happiness. Inside, the very smell of oil, of Mark's tools and sandal leather, injured me with memories that were suddenly painful.

I spent weeks nursing myself back to health in the shadows inside my home. No one came to see me. The interior became a tomb. My reputation brought shame heavily upon me, the reputation of sharing the bed of a heretic.

No one would give me work, and threats came often to my door. Before long, I sold my home and took to the streets with the last of Mark's work, wearing a face scarred and weathered, and a lifetime removed from the simple pleasures of clean feet.

Months passed, becoming years. Not a day went by that I did not sit in my place on Beggar's Row and finger the stitching in the last pair of my beloved husband's sandals. Eventually, I would have to sell them, because rarely did I receive kindness from those passing on the roads.

As I sat one day, watching for a gracious traveler, I saw a familiar man passing by and pulling a handcart filled with wood. He could not help but watch the beggar's as they besought his charity. His eyes gaunt, I knew he had little to give, and so drew my shawl forward that I might not look too pitiful and earn his last coin. I had learned the weakness of the poor to share their means more liberally than the rich, even when it endangered their own survival to do it.

To my surprise, the man paused in the road and came to me. Kneeling down, he took my hand and placed a few mites in my palm. "It isn't much," he apologized. "But it is all I have."

I looked up into his tired eyes. Sweat coated his face, matting his hair. I knew him from somewhere, but still could not place it.

THE BEGGAR

Then he answered the question for me. "I am sorry they took your husband and children from you. I pray you may one day be reunited."

It was then that I recognized him—my sole defender at the hour of my loss. This man wore the face of one unable to part with even a few bronze coins—a condition I knew well. "I cannot take these. You look like you have need of them."

He curled my fingers back over the coins. "I believe my wife would want you to have them. I've got everything I need." Motioning to his cart filled with wood, he gave me a pleasant smile and returned to the road. A moment later, he was gone inside the city.

Thoughtful as it was, the offering lasted me but two days.

A few days since the isolated act of kindness, I held Mark's last pair to my nose and breathed the scent of leather. Over the straps I lifted my eyes toward the horizon to see who would pass next the line of Bethlehem's deserted and hopeless. Up the road came a man leading a woman seated atop a shabby donkey. Seeming weary, the woman's chin rested against her chest, a blue shawl protecting her from rogue winds and their flurries of dust. Though small, she was clearly heavy with child. The man watched his feet as he walked, as if concentrating on each next step. When they drew nearer, I could see the tired creases about his eyes from hours of squinting against the sun and wind.

I judged them a modest couple in every way, and dropped my eyes. This time I would permit no opportunity for my misfortune to play upon the sympathies of the poor, not eve for a mite. I silently prayed the others who begged by my side would let this couple pass without dunning them too severely.

The plod of hooves sounded rhythmically against the wall at my back and rose into the sky above. I pulled my shawl tightly around my left cheek and tucked Mark's sandals beneath my skirt. A mournful cry for alms started at the far end of the row, words lost as they mingled together and drowned out individual meaning.

Askance, I saw the couple spare glances at the poor who petitioned them. A pained look registered in their eyes, and more than once they looked at one another, appearing to share a wish that they had something to give.

I hunkered lower still as they drew abreast of me, keeping only a view of the road that I might take sight of their feet as they passed—an old habit that wouldn't let me alone. In that moment I saw the man's feet caked with the grime of desert sand, and the woman's small, delicate toes beneath the hem of her dress. No sandals did either of them wear.

My heart pounded in that instant. I had known the rough feel of stones on my skin, and the emptiness of loving children I could no longer hold or even see. This frail girl about to begin her family should not tread a dirty street or feel the prick of jagged rocks. Worry erupted in me at the thought that her poverty might displace her and the child she bore into the streets, bringing her nearer to Beggar's Row than a new mother should ever be. And how long had her husband walked the open road and felt the stab of thorns or the indifferent jut of a pebble in his sole? Urgency quickened my heart and would not ease. The feet of a long, long journey. This meant more to me as words swelled up from the past: *I do hope I live to meet the man who uses those feet. I do hope to offer him something to ease the footsteps of his journey.* I did not believe this man to be the messiah, but inside I knew that he and his wife were somehow linked to the advent of our liberation. An irrepressible feeling grew in my heart at the very sight of them. I immediately pulled from my skirt the last tokens I had of my dear husband, and raised my damaged face toward the couple. Urgently, I waved the sandals at them. "Here," I called. "Please, take these for your feet."

The man pulled to a stop. Such attention from travelers on the road usually brought a renewed wave of petitions from the Row. Today, a hush fell over the wall. Slowly, the man led his animal to the side of the road and stopped before me. Kind eyes peered down as I extended the sandals to the limit of my reach. He looked over his shoulder at his wife, who returned a smile to both of us.

The man looked at me, gently took the sandals from my hand and walked back to the packs slung over his animal's back. He produced a water skin from beneath a blanket and came back to where I sat. Kneeling down, he set the sandals to one side and reached for my feet. Shocked, I submitted to his gentle touch.

The man removed my old sandals and placed them to one side. He then poured water over my left foot, softly scrubbing the filth away. Twice he looked up, a thin smile on his lips, never speaking. When he finished cleansing the skin, he dried my foot with the hem of his own garment. Then he took a small vial from his pouch and smoothed a drop of oil over his palms. With great care he rubbed the ointment across my sole, ankle, and toes. The fragrant smell of olive and sage permeated the air. In that moment the yoke of the beggar lifted from my shoulders; I felt free of the losses piled upon me.

The man repeated the process with my other foot, seeming to delight in this small kindness. I did not need to look to see the amazement of my companions on the Row. No such honor had ever been seen here. It was not a coin in my hand, but something much more, a deposit made in the well of my spirit, which had run dry long ago.

When he finished, the man sat a moment, simply staring into my eyes. I had the impression he somehow knew my past from but a look. His thoughtful brow convinced me that he surely would touch the life of Israel's redeemer in some way. So like my Mark he was.

His steady hands took my offering, that last vestige of the man I'd once loved, and placed them on my clean feet.

"They seem just the right fit," he said, smiling.

"But I want you to have them," I countered. "Please, it means more to me than you can know. I have a feeling . . . my husband . . ." I could not finish.

"Good woman," the man began, clasping my feet in his large hands, "Your kindness is your gift to us. That," and he picked up my used sandals, "and this fine pair of sandals here."

He pulled them onto his own feet. "They seem to fit just fine. Mine became unserviceable many days ago—"

"Please take the new ones," I broke in. "They will last much longer. If you could know . . . if you could understand—"

He gently squeezed my feet to silence me. "Dear woman, I should rather walk in the sandals of she who gave what she could not afford to give than stride with the finest workmanship in Judea. Each step I take will remind me that there is forever something more we may offer, something dear that may yet spare the suffering of another." I saw tears threaten to escape his eyes. "When my heart feels trodden upon, and my hope ebbs low in coming to this place to pay my tax; when I bring my wife to bear her child with little to make her comfortable; when all this oppresses my mind and threatens my peace, I will take another step and feel the reminder of you where my skin meets the earth, and remember my instruction from one who had naught to give.

"And this will I teach the child that comes to us soon." With a tremulous whisper he spoke with magnificent gratitude. "No greater lesson may I impart to him. And no greater teacher could I have had than you. Thank you. May Yahweh make His face to shine upon you."

From behind him the woman added softly, "Amen."

He stood, and in parting reached down a hand, drew back my shawl, and tenderly touched my scarred cheek. In the same certain voice that Mark had used when telling me of his impressions of the coming messiah, the man said, "You have sturdy feet, and beauty unsurpassed. Let no shame have place inside you. Your example will surely touch eternity."

Taking up his donkey's tether, he gave a final smile and moved on. I watched him stride away, watched a surer step in my sandals. Never was I so grateful for large feet. I dropped my eyes to my own washed and anointed skin, and Mark's beautiful workmanship stitched across the strapping. Forgotten were my losses, and new hope filled the places where my debt of grief had emptied me. The Row remained quiet, only a few whispers shared amidst a few of its tenants.

A new beginning did I feel, but no rush to move just yet. As night came, I sat against the wall and marveled as my strip of shade during the day became luminous beneath the light of a great star in the dark of night. Things had truly changed. There seemed no darkness that could hold me.

I smiled in the cool evening air, content to consider the many possibilities before me. Sometime later, I heard the hurried feet of someone racing through the night, and presently a man skidded to a halt before me, wearing finely crafted boots. His lungs labored to take air. A delighted look glowed on his features. Appearing as filled with hope as I felt, he put out his hand and showed me a beautiful necklace. I reached up past the jewelry and used his arm to stand. Together we clasped the precious item in our hands and embraced. There was a child somewhere close by that I simply had to meet.

Olive Branch

I grew up walking the hills where my ancestors planted and cultivated the trees for their life-giving fruit. All my life I helped harvest the drupes and accompanied papa to market where we sold them as food and oil. The market was an exciting place, filled with delicious smells, men excitedly bartering, and the most beautiful clothes and woven rugs. But I preferred the groves. I liked to walk beneath the white blooms of the trees that stretched as far as I could see. They reminded me of a cloud resting upon the ground, and spending time there made me feel like I was walking in the sky. That was why I wanted my own grove.

The day I finally convinced Mama to be my advocate for getting my own olive trees, I waited anxiously for Papa to come in from his long day of work. After supper, they went into their room and closed the door. I crept up close to eavesdrop.

"Drupe wants her own grove?" Papa's voice was loud and incredulous. He called me "Drupe" because he said I was his sweetest olive, with the hardest center. Some might have mistaken his tone for anger, instead of the weariness I knew he felt at day's end.

"Ridiculous," continued Papa. "She has enough to do just helping me."

"She's a little girl, David," Mama countered. "She needs to have something to care for. It isn't right that she spends all her time working the groves with you and the other men. Where will she learn to nurture new life? Where—"

"Delilah," Papa cut in harshly, "she has *you* to teach her the ways of womanhood. She needs no tree to do it for her. I can't have her wasting all her time fussing over striplings that bear little fruit, and she isn't old enough to manage crop-bearing trees yet."

"There is plenty of time for her to help you and grow a few small trees," Mama argued back at Papa. A seat creaked as one of them stood. "Since Malachi died, she's had no one her own age to talk to. She needs to feel important to someone or something. She needs to feel depended on. What harm is there in giving her a few trees to care for?" Mama's voice softened. "They might even grow and yield us a crop."

"She has me to talk to!" yelled Papa. His voice always rose when Malachi was mentioned, as though talking more loudly might shut out the memory of his son's death.

It never worked.

"Besides," he went on, "this very kind of foolishness is why Malachi is gone. No boy belongs on the open road when the sun is down. And no girl either."

Anger filled me. I sensed Papa would not be turned from his decision. I felt bad that I'd put Mama in the position of defending me against Papa's 'day-end' voice.

"I won't have my only child playing the part of farmer or Mama ... or son," Papa trumped, "before she is old enough to be responsible and safe. Do you hear me—"

"David," Mama tried to interrupt.

"No, Delilah, you listen to me." I could hear Papa pacing from where I crouched behind the door. "It is better this way. I will teach her to be smart with the merchants. I'll teach her industry, agriculture. She'll be well wed with such skills." The sound of a fist slamming on their bedroom table echoed behind the door. I rose to my feet, my own fists balling up. Suddenly now my wedding was being discussed, and all I'd wanted was a tree of my own! "I'll see her safely out of our home!" Papa's vowed. "And for a dowry I'll bestow a grove of trees nourished on land that's been in my family for generations. That is what will be! Now I will hear no more!"

I burst through the door, unable to listen any more. "You stop talking to Mama that way!" I scolded. "I love her. I won't let you do it anymore!"

I rarely saw such a look on Papa's face. His mouth hung open; his hands froze in mid-gesture. "I know you get tired, we all know it," I continued. "But you make people afraid with your big, loud voice. And you're always yelling, telling us all how it 'will be'! So just stop it! Stop it!" I punctuated my demand by thumping my own small fist on the same table papa had hit.

The room got very quiet. Mama looked at me in utter surprise. Papa looked puzzled, as though he weren't sure whether to laugh at me or take an olive switch to my behind. But I did not back down. I might never get a little grove of my own, but I hated the loud, irritated voice papa used when work was done. I meant to change it.

Finally, Papa dropped his hands, and a smile spread on his wide, chiseled lips.

"You are right, Elizabeth." He perched on the edge of the bed and put his arms out, inviting me to come to him. I stood unmoving, wary. "Still hard," he laughed. "Come little Drupe, I wish to beg your forgiveness."

I went to him slowly, and he hugged me. I sank into his arms and pulled Mama into our embrace.

"You make good peace, Drupe," Papa laughed. "Let us eat, what do you say?" He patted my shoulder and kissed Mama. His voice came softly, a deep, low grumble that managed to sound kind despite its natural coarseness.

I nodded, and the three of us ate olives, cheese, and bread with a lamb broth Mama warmed by the fire. We spoke little, and smiled more than I ever remember. Even Papa. He kept shaking his head as he popped olives in his mouth, each time removing the pit and showing it to me, as though a symbol of who I was. In turn, I lifted bites of cheese toward Papa and munched them hungrily, smiling as I looked at him.

Abruptly, Papa stood, pushing back his chair and finishing a cup of fresh wine. "Talk to me while I make the oil," he invited, heading for the door on his way to his workshop.

I finished my dinner, stuffing three bites into my mouth, and waved goodbye to Mama as I raced after him.

In the workshop were the olives and presses and all the things we use to tend the groves. It smelt strongly of the drupe, but also of wood and polished brass. The light of the lamps flickered over the surfaces, even the pool of oil Papa pressed from the olives. I took my regular stool from the corner and placed it near the barrels. Papa started to feed the olives into the press, and I folded my hands in my lap, waiting.

"What do you want to talk about tonight, Drupe?" he asked.

This was it. My chance. "Papa, I want my own olive grove."

"Let's talk about something else." He finished dumping the olives into the press, and tossed the basket aside.

"I want my own grove," I persisted. "Not one of yours; a new one. I want to plant new trees and raise them myself." I curled my hands into balls and looked into Papa's face.

"Elizabeth, you are too young to tend a grove by yourself. One day you will be married, and your husband will come to live with us and work with me in the trees of our forefathers. You will want children, and we will build you a home." He started to press the olives, apparently thinking he had answered my request.

"No, I want to grow my own trees and harvest my own olives, please." I remained firm, but moderated my tone. I did not want to sound as angry as I had before supper.

Papa stopped his work and squatted down before me. For several moments, he looked deeply into my eyes. Usually, I could tell what he was thinking, but tonight I could sense nothing. A furtive smile played at his lips, but never quite took full form in the set of his mouth. Then a horrible look of regret threatened to pull his eyes and jowls into a frown. A calloused hand came to rest on my own coiled fingers. I had never seen Papa consider something so. In that moment I learned something of him, something more true than the mere fatigue he felt after a day in the trees.

After a long exhalation, he began, "Caring for the olive tree is hard work. Drupe, you must think of *its* needs, *its* health. It will nourish you, but only if you nourish it."

I did not reply, but kept a determined look, understanding that he was not talking me out of my grove.

Papa showed an intent look. "All right, you may have your own grove."

I squealed with joy. At last, my own piece of heaven! I would have my own trees, my own blossoms, my own cloud on earth!

"But we will begin with one tree, Drupe," he continued. "If you show that you can care for one, we will add others. In time, it will be a grove, but we will start by planting one tree."

I nodded eagerly. "You will see, Papa, it will be the best olive grove in all of the land! People will come for miles to buy oil from Elizabeth of Bethlehem."

Papa smiled and stood, working his press again. "You know, Drupe, I think you are just the one to do it."

The very next day we planted my first tree. I did not want any of the other trees mixed up with my own, so I chose a hill far from Papa's trees, and with his help, we started my grove.

Every day for three years I walked to my tree, spoke to it, watered it, and even named it Jeshua. Though small, Jeshua remained healthy. Papa said it would grow into a fine olive tree if I continued to care for it as I had. Papa and I planted two other trees near Jeshua, one each year, but both perished. Undaunted, I kept care over Jeshua as strictly as Papa did over me.

In the autumn of that year, harvest came early, catching Papa unprepared. With little time to take in his crop, he worked longer days than normal. For weeks, I heard him rise while the sun still slept deep behind the mountain. In the quiet of our home, his movements seemed loud, though I could tell he attempted not to wake us. Then, the door would shut quietly, and I would listen as his footsteps disappeared in the early morning dark. I always fell asleep again for what seemed a long time before waking, and even then the sun had not risen into the sky. Only the light blue of twilight lit the horizon as I ate breakfast and thought of what I'd do once I finished my chores.

When night came that harvest season, I was always in bed before Papa came back to the house. From beneath my blankets I listened to him talk with Mama while she put a plate before him. He was losing much of his crop to the heat which had brought an early harvest. The olives had ripened too fast, and many dropped before they could be picked. Others withered on the branches. The endless work of picking, all done beneath a brutal sun, had caused Papa to lose much weight. His face appeared more leathery and wrinkled than ever.

At the end of one of those long, hot days, I returned home in time to carry a bucket of water to Jeshua. Coming through the door, I saw Papa preparing to head back to the groves.

"Drupe," he said, a fatherly smile easing his weathered features, "come with me to the groves. We can talk as we pick a few bushels before bedtime."

"She has not had supper yet," Mama protested.

"Give her some bread and cheese to eat while we walk." Papa ruffled my hair.

"No," I cut in, "I need to water Jeshua. I can't come."

"Your tree will be fine another day," Papa insisted. "As I remember, you took it water yesterday."

"He needs a drink *every* day," I argued.

"Elizabeth, even in this heat a tree does not need to be watered each day." His wisdom dispensed, a smile returned to his lips. "Come, we will talk as we used to do. It has been too long since we discussed our special things." He motioned with his hand and took a step to entice me.

I didn't want to go. I thought I had outgrown those infantile "talks" Papa liked so much. Usually, only he talked and I listened; that was just a lecture. Besides, the heat had sapped my strength, and I didn't relish the thought of spending the last hour of dusk picking olives.

Papa waved at me again.

"Maybe that's why your crop is failing," I said viciously. "Perhaps if you cared for your trees as I do Jeshua, we wouldn't be in danger of going hungry when the season ends." I lifted my chin with deliberate superiority.

The wide expectancy in Papa's eyes slackened.

A knock came at the door. I saw gratitude in Papa's eyes for the intrusion. He went to the door and drew it open. Night having fallen, a spill of light fell in a bright square around Papa's friend Luke, the carpenter.

"Luke, what can I do for you?" Papa asked, running his hand through his hair. He motioned for his friend to enter.

The carpenter's cheeks were hollow. He stepped inside and followed the smell of supper to Mama's pot. Mama wiped her hands on a rag as she regarded Luke with a smile. "How is Ruth?" She asked. "Your child comes soon, if I'm not mistaken."

The carpenter nodded, adding a faltering smile.

After a moment, he turned sheepish eyes back to Papa, as if wanting to ask something, but seeming uncomfortable about it. He dropped his head and muttered the name "Ruth" under his breath. Then, with a more determined eye he looked up and spoke.

"David, I have the opportunity for work, but I need some wood to begin. Can I borrow just a few limbs from you?"

Once the words were out, Luke's face grew paler still. He again dropped his eyes, clenching at a mallet and chisel he held in each hand. As if suddenly aware that he held these items, he raised them toward Papa. "I can give you these in trade."

The hopeful look on the carpenter's eyes silenced everyone. I ceased to fidget, Mama stopped her supper preparations, and Papa stood motionless, as though appraising his friend. I believe Papa was gaining a sense of Luke's need, that he feared to return home if he failed to obtain the object of his errand. It was the same look of worry as I'd seen on Papa's face as he fretted over the harvest of the olives.

A long, awkward moment passed before Papa finally spoke.

With kind eyes, Papa said, "Luke, take what you need."

The carpenter's mouthed opened and closed, but he said nothing, seeming to be too overwhelmed by emotion to speak. The corners of his mouth tugged as though he might weep. He looked at the tools in his hands, gripping them tightly, purposefully. Then, he pulled Papa into a tight embrace and whispered over his shoulder, "I will repay you."

Papa patted Luke's back. "You will have the chance to help me someday. I'm almost sure of it. A carpenter's trade is always in demand, right?" He stood back and scratched at his stubbly chin. "Besides, would I let you forget that you owe me?" A broad smile spread on Papa's lips, revealing a small bit of olive lodged between his lower teeth.

Laughing with him, Luke shook his head. "No, I suppose you wouldn't." They clasped hands and Luke turned toward the groves, nodding toward me and Mama before he stepped into the night.

When he had been gone several moments, Papa turned to me. "There's still time for our talk."

Without thinking, I blurted, "But what about my tree?"

"Your tree will be fine one day without you," Papa replied.

"And so will you," I countered. My anger boiled inside me. I would not let him come between me and my grove. "I certainly would not have given the carpenter permission to take the limbs off one of my trees."

Papa did not raise his 'day-end' voice. He merely turned without a word and trundled toward his groves. Watching him go, I realized something I hadn't considered: our talk might have eased those few hours of work. He was tired and needed my help. Perhaps more than that: he was lonely, and wanted company. I hadn't needed to remind him of the danger our diminished crop portended for us. I'd listened to him rise and return while I enjoyed the comfort of my bed, as he worked to ensure a productive season. Everywhere the heat and drought had taken its toll, and no less so on my Papa. How much wearier must he have been than me, and yet I put my own needs before his. He worked through the baking sun to keep whatever promises he'd made to Mama and me. I held one allegiance: myself.

Ashamed, I raced after him, but stopped just beyond the square of light falling from the door. The smell of harvest lingered in the air, olives collected in bushels, oil presses slick with their work. A warm night breeze blew the fragrance south, a kind of invitation. I breathed deeply of the familiar smell, my feelings suddenly a tangle in my stomach.

Before long, Papa had disappeared among the trees, and I ran toward Jeshua, able to think of nothing else to do.

My regret had almost faded as I rounded the last turn toward my tree. I skidded to a halt in alarm: a small herd of goats milled around my tree, a herdsman asleep not far away. The animals moved and bleated, rooting over the ground for fresh grass to graze. Two of the beasts nibbled at Jeshua's branches.

I tried to scream, but the shock of what I saw robbed me of breath. Quickly, I bent and took up a rock, hurling it at the goats. My aim caused one of them to jump back and cast me a blank stare as it chewed some of Jeshua's leaves in its crooked teeth. The other animal continued to eat my tree, unaffected. I sprinted toward the beast, my voice breaking free as I ran. A great shriek tore from my throat and filled the darkening night with anger. The herdsman awoke at my cry in time to see me tackle the mindless goat.

I pummeled the animal with my tiny fists, glad for every whining bleat it made. The other animals backed away, scattering from around my tree. The herdsman stood, and hurried steps approached me. I paid them no mind, punishing the goat for wounding my little grove.

The awful stench of its breath and tongue brought new anger, and I wrenched on the beast's neck savagely. Suddenly, the goat and I were separated. Instead, I stood looking into the confused and irritated face of the herdsman. He seemed to expect an answer. I gave him one, spitting in his face and trying to kick him.

Holding me at bay, he raised a hand as if to strike me.

"Hold!" The command echoed up the hill, freezing the herdsman's hand in mid-air.

I struggled to look around, and saw Papa coming up the trail at a brisk walk. The herdsman released me, and I fell to the ground. I scampered to Jeshua's side as Papa came to a stop beside me.

"If she's yours," the herdsman said, ire tinting his words, "then you'll want to explain why she attacked my herd. I could have compensation from you for her assault."

Papa said nothing and looked down at me. His attention shifted to Jeshua, then back at the herdsman. "You're a negligent herder, my fellow. Bringing your goats into my orchard. Are you so blind that you did not see this delicate tree here?" Drawing his brows together, Papa focused a stern gaze on the man.

The herdsman stuttered in reply, "That tree there? You can't be serious. It's a weed. My animal is worth a lot more than a large twig growing on a barren hill."

Papa pointed a powerful arm at the herdsman. "And my daughter is worth more than everything you own. Get off of my land, and be quick! If I change my mind about it, I'll take my justice this very night beneath a merciless sky for your hand raised against my child."

I had never heard Papa talk that way before. I dared not move or breathe. The herdsman backed slowly away, drawing his goats with him. After several paces, he quickened his step and the herd followed him down the hill.

When the receding steps could no more be heard, Papa knelt beside me, and together we looked at Jeshua.

"He's going to die, isn't he?"

Papa put delicate hands on Jeshua's torn and chewed branches. He spent several moments inspecting them before turning his heavy eyes toward me. "Your tree's chances are not good, Drupe."

I began to weep.

"But," he added quickly, "we will do all we can. The rest we'll leave to Yahweh."

"What does Yahweh care about one little tree?" I looked at Jeshua's torn bark.

Papa did not answer. He put his hand over mine, just as he'd done the night he agreed to let me have my tree, and started to pray. It was not a short prayer. Twice I opened my eyes as Papa spoke his reverent words, and saw night full and dark around us. On he prayed, his coarse hand over mine, the salty smell of him and his day's labor thick in the air, his gruff voice supplicating Eternal Father. Sometime during that long prayer on my distant hill, I began to believe Jeshua would live. I squeezed Papa's rough fingers, and prayed with him.

Our prayers were answered. Jeshua lived.

A few weeks later, as I walked home from my friend Hezrah's house, a flake floated down on my nose. I wiped it away. A moment later another flake fell on my arm. I studied the ashen bit closely before casting my eyes heavenward. A rain of similar flakes fell lazily, filling the sky with darkness and soot. Though I'd never seen it, Papa had told me about the rain of fire. I ran and soon saw in the distance a fiery glow on the hill. Gritty pieces of the ashen rain got into my eyes and mouth. The ground plumed with each running stride I took, and the blaze upon the meadows grew brighter, the air hotter.

I got to our home and saw Mama putting things on a cart harnessed to our mule. Papa knelt at the edge of the workshop. He was praying, and crying, his hands outstretched to catch the ashen waste that was all that remained of his olive groves. Up the hill, great fires swept the last of the trees, consuming them quickly. Suddenly, I thought of Jeshua.

I raced from the house, ignoring Mama's warnings. I ran as fast as I could, and tripped on a rock, scraping my hand as I scrambled up the incline of the hill. I ignored the cut in my palm and got to my feet, running again to protect my tree.

As I came around the final hill, I saw that Jeshua still stood. The fires had not passed along the brush of the ground and consumed him. I quickly cleared the area of plants and wood, and fashioned a wide ring of rocks around him. Then I sat on the ground to watch the continuing rain of burnt olive leaves. In my heart I felt both pain and relief. Papa's orchards were burnt to nothing, but my tree was safe. I wondered if Papa would take my tree. Sitting there, I began a vigil to guard Jeshua as much from Papa as from the fire.

Several hours later, Papa found me asleep, curled around Jeshua's thin trunk. He carried me home, and the lingering scent of fire and ashes grew stronger with every step he took. I fell to sleep beneath my covers that night to the muted sounds of Papa and Mama crying behind their door.

Two nights later a knock came at our door. "David, it's me, Matthew. Please, let me in. I have news."

Papa went to the door. His sandals leaving new bits of ash to speckle our floor. The smell of smoke cloaked everything. He opened the door and Matthew's bright, animated face shone in at us. Mama did not greet him, but continued to prepare our supper.

"What is it, Matthew? This is not a good time." A bitter stare twisted Papa's words into a snarl.

"It is the coming of our deliverance! Forget your orchard. All will be made new." Enthusiasm poured from Matthew's wide eyes and hurried speech, enticing us to be caught in its happy contagion. Papa only sighed and retired to his chair.

Matthew stepped in, closing the door behind him.

"Unless you can bring my trees back from the ashes," Papa said, pointing at the ashes on the floor, "don't talk to me of deliverance."

Matthew quickly took a chair and sat beside Papa. "It is come to pass, David! Born this very night in Bethlehem is the Christ! An angel has appeared to the men in the fields and spoken these very words."

Once again I saw the look upon Papa's face. I was glad to see it. Since the fires, the soot seemed always to be on his cheeks, and angry thoughts constantly drew his lips into a frown. But now, his jaw dropped and his eyes seemed to see things far away.

Mama stopped her preparations and drew close.

"Yes, David, it is so," Matthew affirmed. "Even now, as I sit here speaking to you, a babe is nestled in the stable at Michael's inn. In the night sky a great star shows the path that leads to his bed. This

PETER VANCE ORULLIAN

is the miracle we have been waiting for! Come with me! I go now, to greet him." Matthew rose.

Papa stood, his body trembling as he struggled to issue commands. "Elizabeth, put out the fire. Delilah, prepare a fresh bowl of olives to present . . ." His voice faltered. There were no fresh olives to prepare, his crop having been destroyed when fire took the storage buildings along with the orchards. Papa sat down heavily and cupped his face in his hands. "Our messiah finally come, and I have no olives of which to make a gift to him."

Mama put her hand on Papa's shoulder, and Matthew quietly opened the door. "David, you should come. He is but a babe and could want nothing from you. Don't delay. Prepare your family, and come look upon the baby king." He did not wait for a reply, but stole off into the night.

As he left, I went to the window and searched for the star of which Matthew spoke. I did not have to look long. It gleamed bright and beautiful, touching the edges of everything with a great silver light. Papa had sometimes spoken of the meanings in the stars. He'd often lain in the grassy meadow beside our home and nestled me beside him as he pointed to the glimmering lights. At the ends of his fingers, I identified those bits of heaven, and learned of the reverence Papa kept for the sacred. Looking back at him sitting with his face cupped in his hands, love swelled in my narrow chest for a man who toiled in the earth and soil of this ancestral home, but regarded with such wonder and respect the holy symbols set high in the sky.

I jumped to my feet. "Papa, we are going! You and Mama prepare yourselves and head toward the city. I will catch up."

"Elizabeth, hush, child! We are destitute. We have lost everything. Please, sit down." He spoke through the fingers cradling his brow.

"No! I will not. You had better do as I say, because I will soon be on the road to Bethlehem to find this baby, and you wouldn't want anything to happen to me as I walk alone in the night." I leapt to the door and dashed away before Papa could catch me. He called after me, but I did not heed his cries.

In moments, I had reached Jeshua. The shining star illuminated him with a warm glow. I sat near his small trunk, just inside the circle of stones, and spoke to him.

"Jeshua, I know you haven't yet borne any olives for harvest, but there is a greater need tonight than for mere drupes. I do not wish to harm you, but your branches are all that are left of Papa's orchard. I must take one to give to this babe. Do you understand?" My words were soft, but so still was the air that I could hear them reaching well into the hills.

I waited as though my tree might reply. I surveyed every part of each small branch, tentatively touching some. The scars from the goats could still be seen. But the light of the star above made everything appear new, fresh. It frosted the ash from my Papa's burning trees, giving everything a delicate look, like new-fallen snow. I hesitated to cut a branch from Jeshua's young trunk. As I waited to know if I should really do it, I looked back the way I'd come, and saw my own footprints in the ash. I remembered Papa walking here with me to plant my first tree for my own grove. The leaves, bark, and branches of Papa's olive trees—his life—coated the world around me, and only my tree had been spared. When I told Papa to stop yelling, he had done so. When I asked for my own tree, he had given it to me. When I refused to help him harvest his crop, instead to tend my own growing orchard, he'd said nothing of his own weariness or need, and let me go. Then, when at last he'd come to find me that night, he'd knelt with me and prayed over my tree.

Lovingly, I removed one of Jeshua's limbs and said a prayer that my tree would mend. Then, I ran toward Bethlehem.

I knew where Michael's stable was located. He always bought a great many olives from Papa for his inn. Finding the stable wouldn't have been difficult anyway. The bright star seemed to guide me, and a crowd of people gathered at its entrance. Papa and Mama stood to one side, looking in toward the manger.

I ran to them and pulled at Papa's sleeve. "Here, give him this." I handed Papa the olive branch. Papa took Jeshua's limb. He nearly dropped it, his fingers trembling mightily as he took hold of it. "Elizabeth, is this—"

"It's all right, Papa. I know Jeshua would want it this way. I was careful, and he will heal. Now you can give the baby this branch. It is not as good as olives, but it is what olives come from. And I think he'll understand."

"Little Drupe," Papa murmured, his voice quavering. "Thank you." He bent and kissed me tenderly, tears glistening in his eyes. He then took me by the hand and led me past the others to the soft lamplight of the inner stable.

We waited a moment together, and Papa wiped his eyes. He placed the olive branch in my hand and clasped my small fingers gently with his own large palms. When we laid Jeshua's limb at the foot of the cradle, I thought I could smell the sweet fragrance of olive groves. In that moment, I knew my grove would flower one day, and that our family would walk together beneath an earth-cloud of drupe blossoms.

Father's Vineyard

My father had grand plans for me. Tutors came daily to lead me in an array of lessons, from history, mathematics, and oration, to music, painting, and poetry. Papa desired that I would rise to an office in Caesar's court. Stubbornly unrefined that I was, it seemed no lesson ever began without papa pulling straw from my hair or running a washcloth under my nose and over my chin to wipe away grape stains.

"These are the finest instructors money can buy," he'd intone impatiently. "Several jugs just to secure a week of instruction. I know you're just nine, Julius, but you must pay attention if you are to do more with your life than raise grapes."

Usually I ignored his complaints, gazing past him to the fields and barns, hoping he wouldn't notice my dirty, bare feet. Most of my life I seemed only to be his frustration. He cultivated his parcel of Etrurian land to produce one of Rome's finest wines, whilst I eluded him at every opportunity to play with the animals in the stables or run the furrows between the grapevines.

One afternoon, I stepped from the house and saw Papa engaged in conversation with two men in clean, white togas. Spotting me, he called me over.

"This is my son, Julius," he announced proudly, as I ambled up, munching a bunch of grapes.

Papa looked down at me, a frown tugging his mouth and brow taut. I knew that look; it meant my cheeks bore smudges, and my mouth the grime of juice I hadn't bothered to wipe away. Brusquely, Papa tousled my hair, probably hoping to casually clear the bits of hay from my head. I looked up at the visitors and plopped another grape in my mouth.

"Hello," I mumbled through a mouth of sweet pulp.

"This, then, is the boy in training?" one man questioned stiffly.

"He is, Gaius" Papa admitted. A firm hand on my shoulder prompted me to quickly gulp my bite and stand straighter.

"Decorum lessons have yet to begin, I would imagine," the second man commented arrogantly. "This one will need some polish if you expect our recommendation for military service in the finest army the world has ever known. Your vintages will earn you the opportunity, Brutus, but the child will appear as a . . . withered grape, sour to the taste, if his manners are as brusque in the ranks of Caesar's army. A political career begins with courtesy."

"I assure you, Nius, the boy has great promise." Papa smiled proudly. "Already I have had to contract teachers with more skill because my son grows bored from the ease of his assignments. He'll no doubt make a fine addition to the civility and purpose of Roman expansion." He bowed deferentially to the Roman squires.

Gaius chuffed mildly, rocking onto his toes before settling back to earth. He appeared to disdain the need to tread with other mortals. "Perhaps," he said. Then, a curious smile drew one corner of his mouth up in a sardonic curve. "So bright is he that you would have no objection to our submitting some questions to him?" Gaius' brow arched dangerously.

Papa nervously cleared his throat. I grew weary of my tutors to be sure, but not from greatness of intelligence as he claimed.

Nius stooped a little toward me, causing his striped amulet to swing out from his chest in short arcs. He attempted an ingratiating smile. "You've no objection, do you, Julius?"

I shrugged, hiding my trepidation by taking another nibble of fruit.

"There, then," said Nius. "He certainly bears his confidence well, if with a touch of indifference. Let us begin." He leveled his gaze at me. "Son, who is our current Emperor and Lord?"

I licked my lips. "I think his name is Caesar."

"Yes, yes, of course he is!" the man spat with impatience. "But his family name, you must possess this prevailing knowledge, living under an Etrurian roof?"

I looked at both men, then my papa. No help was forthcoming. "Well, I hear the name Augustus all the time. I will guess that is his name." I smiled and rewarded myself with a large grape. A squirt of juice splashed right on the stooping Roman's nose and cheek.

I felt Papa's hand tighten on my shoulder. I'm not sure if it was because I'd soiled the man's skin or because I'd guessed the wrong name. Or maybe because I'd guessed at something I should have rightly known. I remained straight and tall, keeping my eyes fixed ahead of me as papa had taught me. I'm certain the Roman emissaries thought me impudent.

"One might *guess*," Nius remarked acidly, "that your son is not the prodigy you describe, but more a rustic, well-suited to the labors of the soil." He glared at me. "And what glory ought to touch the lips of every senator, merchant, every . . . vintner, my boy? Tell me."

This time I thought longer, trying to recall something from the endless lessons I had daydreamed through. A panic washed over me, and I stole a glance toward the stables. When I looked back, baleful eyes met my own, impatient and demanding. "I think . . ." I stammered.

"Do no such thing, boy!" Nius interjected. "It is sure knowledge this. You live it, breathe it every day. Come! Do not hesitate!"

I forgot to chew the rest of my mouthful of grapes. And I could not meet Papa's eyes. I just wanted to run, get to someplace safe, flee those judging eyes. Beneath them I felt low, stupid. They knew I didn't know the answer. Yet they would make me respond anyway, force me to humiliate myself. More than that. It would embarrass Papa; I would let him down. I didn't want to upset him, but the high ceilings of Rome, its ornate handicrafts, its order and dignitaries meant nothing to me. Better to me were the fields, the smell of budding vines, sweet hay laid up in the barns, and talking to the animals stabled for the night.

When I could delay no longer, I said, "The glory of a good wine."

Caustic laughter ensued. It came at my expense, but an awkward moment of real humor tempered the reality of my error. The smiles faded when the men realized I had not meant my response as a joke.

It was Gaius' turn to lean toward me. His heavily creased face, folding on itself like an old sow's skin, frowned menacingly. "Brutus," he addressed Papa, not faltering in his rapt stare into my eyes. "I will begin more fundamentally even than these basic questions. For the sake of your tenure upon this land, despite the homage you pay Rome with your product, we hope this child does not fail to identify our most primary concern."

His robes shifted as he took half a step closer. "Son, what hope do you bear, what feeling do you have about your own life, its purpose, your place as a citizen of this noble empire?" He narrowed his eyes. "I ask, you see," he forced a conversational tone, "because each of us has aspirations, ideas about what we'd like to be when we grow up, the things we'd like to do with our lives." His manner darkened. "Your father has lobbied us quite convincingly on your behalf that your future is bright in the circles of Roman influence. With some tribute and his finest bottles we have been persuaded to secure a station for one son of an Etrurian vintner. So you see, young man, it is simply natural that we would like to have your thoughts upon the topic of your own life's path."

A thousand answers coursed through my head. I sensed that there must be one perfect response, but I did not know it. I wanted to share the feelings in my heart, but these had never been in alignment with Papa's desires. So, I determined to say the things I believed they wanted to hear. Yet under the weight of their stare, I could not speak. My mouth grew dry. I prayed something would occur to me because I could not delay my reply any longer, but my tongue only clucked against my teeth, thick and numb. I stammered as I watched disapproval blossom in their faces. Papa's grip relaxed on my shoulder; the light feel of disappointment was painful through my tunic.

I turned and ran, racing with all my might for the stable. Not looking back, I burst through the doors and rushed to the far corner, where I cast myself facedown on a great pile of hay. Breathing openly through my mouth, I drank in the peace I had always found there.

I don't know how long I lay there in my grief, but when I finally turned over, the violet hues of dusk showed through the cracks in the walls. Several moments passed before I realized Papa sat quietly nearby. Crouched on a low milking stool, Papa wore eyes heavy with the threat of tears. I sensed that he wanted to say a great many things, but he never spoke. He only sat, occasionally looking up toward the peak of the rafter and down again. I tried to say something, to apologize, but the words would not come.

Sometime after full dark, my dog, Fides, wandered in and snuggled beside me in the hay. His presence somehow made me feel complete, and I began to drift. Papa came over to gently pull several armfuls of hay over me to keep me warm. Without a word, he left the stable.

I awoke the next morning with a sense of calm I hadn't felt before. I lay enjoying the sweet smell of hay, the lowing of the cows, and the quite stillness all around. Nearby, Fides awaited what fun we would find in another turn of the sun. I could fairly smell grapes drawn fresh from the vine.

A twinge of pain struck me at the thought of the prior day's confrontation. But quickly I imagined those great pontificators drunk on our wine and slipping off their thrones. I found comfort in the thought that they were just as human as the rest of us.

Papa's loss of me rising to political station turned out to be his gain in the wine trade. I eventually discovered I was an excellent judge of good wine, and powerfully convincing as a salesman. Growing up so close to the work, I learned something more: to judge a man by the size of the sweat-stain at the armpit of his tunic. Never mind the perfumes the men of the court wore. I preferred the salty smell of real work.

My favorite place remained the same all those years, with the animals we kept, the animals that fed us and were used to cultivate the soil from which we harvested the grapes. I don't believe a day passed that I did not lounge there with my dog in the evening, eating grapes and just breathing the balmy, evening air. The company of animals always made me feel at home, and the sweet smell of grasses lying upon the floor filled the room with a pleasant and comforting musk.

Our vineyard made Papa, Mama and me very wealthy. Yet it wasn't by selling expensive bottles to Caesar and his court that we made our fortune. It was by selling the dregs to everyone else.

At the age of twenty I took to the road with more than a hundred amphora jugs of our stock, embarking upon all the known trade routes. To help me protect my investment, I rode with scurrilous men upon the highways of the plains. I sang bawdy tunes with sailors as I worked back and forth across the Mediterranean. If a man hasn't shouted ribald sea tunes from the side of an ocean-faring vessel with men of the sea, he hasn't experienced the power of song, I say. My education became complete in the company of such fellows, and in a manner the tutors of my youth could never have achieved nor approved of.

Wherever I went, I always first sought the district where the inhabitants' tunics bear the largest sweat stains. Those fellows always drink with the most voracity and sang with the most volume. More often than not, those same fellows bellowed such attempts at song as to encourage my envy of the deaf. However, their thirst was always high because the fluid poured from them during the day. I could always make the trip profitable by selling enough in those areas of Caesar's empire that anything the wealthy contingent purchased beyond that was simply froth on the goblet.

One of the cities I visited was Bethlehem.

I arrived at a meager inn, and went straight to the stables to unburden my horse. The men traveling with me pulled into the shade of several trees and drew themselves each a cup of wine. I left them to their hard-earned refreshment, and noticed a man standing a few paces off, staring in at me.

"What can I do for you?" I asked.

A concerned look pulled the fellow's face into a scowl. "Nothing for me, unless you've got work for a carpenter's skill."

"I'm afraid I can't help you there." I placed my saddle on a large rock and stood up to stretch. The man's eyes never left a manger standing to one side of the stable.

"Your horses pull a wagon filled with Roman amphora jugs and casks," the carpenter said. "Do you mean to do business with the owner of the inn?" A hint of distaste flashed in his eyes.

I strode to the entrance of the hillside stable and looked across at the inn. "That was my intention. Do you know him?"

Finally, the man ended his vigil on the manger, and turned scrutinizing eyes on me. "I do. He is a shrewd businessman to be sure." He eyed me up and down. "You're Roman, so you may fare better than I did."

I tried to coax a smile from the tradesman, having learned that trust follows only after two men can share some levity. "Or perhaps I'll lose my stock and work my way back across the sea," I replied. "The men of Israel know their weight in coin."

The carpenter took another long look at the stable, pausing unduly on the small feedbox. "I caution you to fix a price and gather your payment before making good on your end of the bargain." With that, he turned and strode away, anger and abasement equally measured in his gait.

Fairly warned, I crossed the yard and entered the inn by its front door. A kind woman rented me a room for a meager sum. I stowed my personal belongings before making my way to the common room where food and drink could be found for an equally meager price. The proprietor had made no real attempt at decoration, leaving the walls virtually bare, the tables rough hewn and unstable. The lingering aroma of yesterday's meals caused my mouth to water. I took a seat near the wall and drew a bottle of my own wine.

Shortly, a frail man with a gaunt face approached wearing an oversized apron. He bore the unmistakable look of ownership: overworked, distracted, constantly on the edge of anger.

One other patron occupied the common room, the hour being too early to begin preparations for evening's supper. When the owner stopped at my table, I spoke quickly to set the tone of our conversation.

"Please sit with me a moment. You appear tired, and the hour is slow enough to merit the rest." I gestured to the empty room.

The man raised a dubious brow, then cast an eye over the barren tables as though he'd not noticed them before. Without a word, he sat opposite me. I took the liberty of setting a cup before him, likewise placing one near myself. I poured us each a liberal cup and set my bottle aside.

"Join me in a drink, my friend." I took my cup in hand and raised it beneath my chin. "I'll guess you are the proprietor here, and to your health I'll raise a toast."

A skeptical smile ensued as the man picked up his cup and tipped it to scrutinize the contents. "No man pours free drink who doesn't expect something in return." He sniffed the wine.

"True as day follows night." I took a sip of my drink. "And the cup you hold is filled with the product I hope to sell you. But before you begin with your excuses, or prepare to haggle my price, I want to say two things." He eyed me with suspicion and held the cup further from his lips. "First, I'd like you to taste my wine before you argue over its merits." I paused, baiting the man as I began a relationship of confidence that would serve us both in the future.

He hid his eagerness well. "And the second thing?"

I smiled. "Only to tell you with all sincerity that I like a man who works his own trade, will wear an apron, and whose armpits show me the toil of his labors."

After a moment, the man laughed and took a healthy gulp of my wine. He betrayed himself in an expression of appreciation, and I knew we'd do business to our mutual profit.

"I'm Michael," he said, "and you do indeed make a fine bottle of wine." He shook his head. "But I suspect it comes at too high a price for the clientele I take here. Travelers, passersby, and overland traders tight with their purses, don't savor their drink as much as seek it by quantity to wash the dust from their throats."

"I am Julius," I responded, extending a hand in friendship. "But my friends call me Grape. And I am sure we will meet on a price that lets us both serve our interests and become friends." I refilled his cup, and we talked about the news in Bethlehem and my travels over the trade routes. Our bottle was gone when he stood to begin his supper preparations. "I'll sit here tonight, if you've no objection," I told him. "My pleasure is the people my work allows me to meet."

"By all means," he smiled. "And you may carry in a few casks of your wine. We'll settle on a price later." He waited to see if the arrangement would stir any distrust from me. I thought of the carpenter's words, and considered demanding payment first. Looking into Michael's lean features, I guessed it would end our civility and squelch the deal.

Instead, I laughed and countered. "Throw in a room for the night, Michael, and you'll find me a generous man."

"Done." He stood and began wiping tables on his way back to the kitchen.

I loaded the wine into his storage area, then situated my things in a room before retaking my seat and setting a fresh bottle of wine on the table. Shortly, men began to fill the common room, buying up the last available beds for the night, and calling for plates of food. Before long, night had fallen, and the room rang with loud voices: some arguing, some laughing from deep in their chests, and others calling for more food and drink.

The smell of work came in waves, pushed by the bodies of large men rushing outside to relieve themselves. The common area teemed with occupants, civility largely put aside, the concern of gain momentarily suspended. In the company of such men and women I felt wholly comfortable, though I often remained only an observer. I don't think they had any idea how much money I had. I dressed deliberately to disguise my success.

I did not remain an observer for long.

"Thomas says he can answer any question we put to him," a short, puffy man announced, rising up to stand on his chair so that all might see and hear him. "What's more, he contends that such an ability qualifies him for Emperor. Now, in the spirit of fairness, I say we give him the opportunity to prove this ability and his entitlement to the vaunted position of Caesar."

A corpulent fellow stood, steadying himself against the edge of the table. I could see no less than three open bottles of my wine topple as he did so. They were empty. "It is true. And more!" he proclaimed, stabbing a finger straight up into the air. "Anyone that can confound me will earn my undying devotion. And," he fumbled for one of the overturned bottles, "a free bottle of this beautiful drink, which he may share at my table." He hiccoughed, and sat heavily.

The man standing on his chair shook his head, his lips sliding into an inebriated grin. "Well said. Now, who will begin?"

"I will!" shouted a man from the corner.

"What is your question for our heir to the throne?"

The fellow in the corner stood, puffing his chest in preparation to speak. "I'd like to know what he would do about our taxes. I can hardly support myself, and I've got a wife and child besides." The man slurred his final words, practically falling back into his seat.

"I'll wager your financial difficulties reside in the number of empty cups upon your table," scoffed the man atop the chair. "But your question is a valid one. Let us have an answer." He pointed an accusing finger at the would-be Emperor, who took his lips from his own cup and stood again to reply.

"Taxes ... let's see. Currently, taxes come by way of ... I mean, each man is accountable for ... or rather, it is the responsibility of those who by trade earn a ...." He scratched his head and sat down.

A roar of laughter filled the common room.

"A reasonable answer to so confusing an issue," said the little, puffy man, still perched on his chair like a jocular owl. "Who will try our man's intellect next?"

"Me!" came a female voice from the kitchen, the bark resounding above the din of the crowd. "I've something more in keeping with the heir's mental capacity." She sauntered up to Thomas, pushing her face into his. "I'd like to know if he can successfully call a sheep gone astray. Because the good Lord knows his skills to tend herd aren't what brought that scent to his neck." She sniffed at him, souring her face at his stench.

Another roar of laughter went up. Before the fat man could answer the question, bleats and sheep-calls filled the room. With each person trying to drown out the others, the chorus deafened me. I clasped my hands over my ears, while tears of hilarity wetted my cheeks. Never before had I seen such jovial folks, and most of them drunk on the wine I had brought to Bethlehem.

When their own laughter and fun prevented them from continuing the sheep-calling contest, Thomas arose in affected majesty and drew all eyes to him. When the chuckles settled, and attention had been captured, he strode to the wall and swept the room with a stern gaze. With a quick turn he dropped to his hands and knees, butting his head against the wall and bleating like a cornered sheep. His head cracked repeatedly against the wood, interspersed with his mewling whines. The ensuing uproar might have lifted the roof from the walls. Everyone nodded at his winning sheep-call, acknowledging his qualification for Emperor. When Thomas stood again, he rubbed his head, wincing noticeably.

The room grew sultry with sweat and heat. Hot food came to give energy to a second round of questions. Fingers greedily snatched pieces of flatbread and meat, and slices of sweet vegetables and fruits, creating a slight lull before the next question came.

"Tell us, Emperor, how does one attain the title of Senator in your illustrious court?"

Thomas stood again, waving the roasted leg of a bird and chuffed something unintelligible. Having remained silent long enough, I took the opportunity to jump to my own seat. "A senator gains his seat through a mandate of the masses," I announced. "He represents a segment of the population, expressing their interests to the governing body, and working solutions that meet the needs of the people and the glory of Rome. Which," I pointed to my backside, "can be measured by the padding of one's seat."

Heads turned, mouths fell open. I knew I'd either offended everyone, or spoken far outside their understanding. The answer had come unbidden to my mouth; the product of many tutors paid for by my papa's vineyard. That and a little insolence.

Just when I was preparing to duck what I was sure would be a barrage of food and plates, cheers rang out: "A new contender for Emperor!"

"Someone with real answers!"

"All this, and he makes wine, too."

Instantly, I had a room full of friends. Even Thomas bowed, deferring to me. For an hour I stood on my chair, fielding questions one by one. I mixed fact with fancy, delighting my crowd and my patrons. I won the hearts of good men and women, whose sweat stains showed honesty more boldly than I'd ever seen.

Once in a while, my orations were interrupted by the enchanting sound of a woman's palm lashing across a patron's face for becoming too bold with his hands. Mostly, I liked how everyone in these places laughed together, even when they didn't understand the joke.

"How shall a mother determine the merits of a suitor for her daughter's hand?" one woman sang out above the crowd.

"Fine woman," I lavished, "It is a simple matter. A woman deserves a man who works, but retains his grace. So every mother should stand the hopeful bridegroom beside the hindquarters of an ass. Whichever makes a peep first is not . . . patient enough to deserve the lady's hand."

Raucous laughter ensued.

"And what of war, Emperor?" asked another. "How can Israel be sure your interests are to protect us from our enemies? What advantage lies in the occupation of a handful of desert tribes?"

The crowd attended me more quietly. I passed my eyes over them with deliberation. "I presume you hold yourselves steadfast in the ways of your prophet Moses, and look forward to one who will again lead you from the captivity you believe Rome forces upon you. And perhaps you're right. Rome's interest is its own expansion; to spread the ideal of its principles as widely as possible. Is this not the same hope you harbor in your messiah?" I paused after such an obviously rhetorical question. "Rome will protect you because it claims you," I continued. "Your empty pockets prove their hold upon you." General disgruntlement stirred among them, so quickly I added, "But I claim you and will protect you because you buy my wine with money earned by hard work."

Admiration ascended in a robust chorus of cheers.

When the shouts had died down again, a woman called, "Then tell us! What will you do to ease the burden on our backs and fill the purses at our hips?"

"Why, I'll do what all good Emperors do," I retorted. "I'll tell you it doesn't hurt, raise your taxes, and ask you how you like the improvements."

On it went into the evening. Gradually, the participants became more sedate, and I passed the torch back to Thomas, who received questions affably, but spoke in milder tones. Most of the guests had retired to their rooms, a few leaving for home. While I sat quietly, appeased, listening to Thomas deliver his inaugural speech to his only two remaining constituents, a soft rapping came at the door.

I watched Michael bustle past Thomas and his friends to the front door. Murmured conversation ensued. I tried to ignore Thomas and his effulgent speech about free wine for every one of his subjects now that he was in power. Finally, the door closed and Michael stepped back into the room, looking frustrated. I supposed that he was upset with Thomas for continuing his pageantry while so many were already trying to sleep. I took leave of my august company and went to Michael to discover the matter.

"Who was at the door?" I asked.

"Ah, Grape, it was just some man and his wife wanting a room," he replied. "At this hour, can you believe it? The gentleman's wife was with child, but I have no rooms left."

The thought of turning away a pregnant woman into the night seemed to weigh heavily upon him. Michael looked over my shoulder at Thomas, who was trying to cajole his friends to hoist him onto their shoulders so he could look down upon his kingdom. His followers relented and attempted to lift him. I turned in time to see Thomas, halfway to his place upon their shoulders, go tumbling to the ground. All three men laughed from their seats upon the floor.

"Quiet in there!" Michael shouted. "I'll throw you out if you don't make an end of it."

A thought suddenly occurred to me, something from my childhood. I caught Michael's attention with a touch at his elbow. "The stable."

He looked back at me, irritated. "What?"

"Put them in the stable, Michael. It's dry and warm. You and I both know they won't get a room anywhere tonight."

He paused, then his features softened, as if the suggestion had eased his guilt at having turned the travelers away. "Another inspired answer from the Emperor of the Grape," he muttered. Hurriedly, he opened the door and rushed out into the night. Moments later, he returned, a thin smile on his lips. "Thank you, thank you," he enthused.

I shook my head. "Not at all." Something more occurred to me, and as Michael prepared to pass, I took hold of his arm. "It is a fine stable, Michael. Do you owe any of its comforts to an unpaid carpenter?"

Surprise mushroomed on his face. "I had forgotten! Your reminders are a blessing!"

Again I shook my head. "Glad to be of service."

Michael clapped me on the shoulder. "Thank you. I'll gather the carpenter soon, but first . . ."

He brushed passed me and went directly to Thomas, hoisted the man on his scrawny back, and began to caper and prance about. "Hail Caesar!" he shouted, so cheerful that he forgot his own admonition to be quiet. The four of them laughed and danced and vied for preeminence as each took turn at being Emperor.

I went to the door and watched the man and his pregnant wife make their way to the stable. It wasn't until years later that I learned who they were, when a man by the name of Paul came to my vineyard and taught of the child the woman bore that night. Had I known, I would have given them my room. As it is, I think the child had the better of it. My most blessed moments were lying upon a bed of hay and imagining the future as a boy in my father's vineyard. I like to think the child felt the same.

The Manger ~ Part II

Walking my cart into the gathering dusk beyond the gates of Bethlehem, I carried Ruth's hopeful smile in my mind like a beacon. More than my wife, she had become my only reason to carry on in the face of such hardships as had beset us.

The embarrassment of asking to do free work for Michael, the innkeeper; the scorn of my fellow tradesmen for doing so; and Ruth, herself, deeming my first attempt at building the manger to be inadequate, these things faded when I considered the trust she placed in me, and the life of our unborn child.

Mild evening breezes swept the land, freshened with the scent of cedars. Around me, the world stretched to meet the sky; ahead, the road led to my last chance to procure the wood I needed to complete the job. I breathed deeply, my pace quickening as I recalled a wood castle I tried to sell at market, shelves I removed from an elderly woman's shop that I'd had to use to build a coffin for another man's mother, and the harsh tongue of a money lender who would spare me no loan.

With Ruth grown so weak from lack of food, my fears pressed in around me, and I moved even faster through the night, thinking of promises.

Having given the last of our money to a beggar on the Row, there was nothing left to do but go to my friend David the olive farmer and seek his charity. I arrived to the whir of crickets and the sweet perfume of ripe olives. My old friend was gracious, and willingly lent me what I needed.

I hastened home, and that same evening I worked well into the night. Ruth brought me more to eat, then finally went to bed, exhausted. For my part, I had never felt so awake, so alive, so determined. I planned my work, envisioned the contours. I chuckled at my own earnestness as I considered that I was only fashioning a feedbox for a low-class inn. But it didn't seem to matter. Every stroke of my blade and chisel, each refining notch, every last measurement was as exact as I could make it. I would either be the greatest fool to produce work for free, or the most noted carpenter for animal furniture ever known. Neither mattered. All I cared about was the opinion of the woman that snored mildly from our bed. Into the night I continued my work, smiling at the one indelicate sound my noble, beautiful wife ever produced. Glad of it, I went on. If she slept as sound and calm as an angel, I might have suspected I was in the wrong house.

I finished at dawn.

Quietly, I woke my snoring beauty. With my hands over her eyes, I guided her to my workbenches. Morning freshened the world, glorious hues lighting the east. I removed my hands to let her see the manger.

"Open your eyes," I told her.

Ruth looked. No sooner had she seen the feedbox than she threw her arms around me and hugged me so hard I thought I might collapse from lack of breath. Then, she kissed me, talking as she put her lips on mine. "I love you, Luke! You make me so proud to be your wife. And you are going to get that job." Her unerring hope became my triumph that morning as we embraced over a stable trough.

Still holding on to me, she jumped up and down with excitement, and we lost our balance and fell, just missing the manger. Over the cool earth we rolled, laughing 'til we cried. It seemed so silly, yet entirely appropriate. Somehow the journey had ended, and what happened thereafter didn't matter. Though we hoped this small olivewood box would convince the innkeeper and answer our prayers, I found myself praying as Ruth and I rolled that I would never forget the lesson she had taught me.

I delivered the box that day. The innkeeper was out, but I left the manger in his stable and decided to return later. Days passed, and I still hadn't caught up with Michael to have his decision on giving me the rest of the work. I visited the stable alone twice, staring in at my manger, but unable to gather enough courage to do more than look, grumble at those unfortunate enough to be using the stable, and make my way home empty-handed.

My stomach grew louder each day with hunger, but I tried to ignore it when I heard Ruth's own stomach cry for food. All the while, she talked and sang a happier song than she had for months. Those next few days were enough to wear out my patience, and cause me to doubt the propriety of the good feelings I'd had in crafting the manger. I only hoped Ruth's faith was not misplaced.

That night the innkeeper came to our door. "I want you to come with me," he said.

Before I could ask if he had decided about the rest of the contract, he left our door and headed back toward his inn. I called for Ruth and we quickly followed.

As we came to the inn, we went to the stable where a small crowd of people had gathered. I feared that I had done something wrong and that somehow my manger had implicated me in something. I took Ruth's hand tightly in my own and we crept slowly through the assembly toward the inner stable.

Coming through those gathered around, I saw the most amazing thing I had ever seen in my life. Beneath two oil-lamps lay my manger, a child upon a bed of straw within. His parents knelt behind him, and all those standing nearby looked on in wonder and worship.

"What is this?" I asked in a hushed voice.

"Luke, I am not sure," Michael whispered reverently. "Some are calling this babe a king. Others have just gathered and watched. But whatever the truth, after I told them they could stay in my stable, I returned to find that the woman had given birth and placed the babe there." He pointed at my manger.

THE MANGER - PART TWO

Quietly, we stared in wonder. Ruth squeezed my hand, and I turned to her.

"It is the messiah," she said, her voice certain and melodic. She nodded once, her eyes glassy, catching the light of the oil lamps. "I just know it is! Can't you feel it?" She looked at me expectantly and smiled.

I waited, not knowing how to respond. My mind returned to several images in mild succession . . . I remembered laboring through the night on the box, making sure lines and tight seams. I remembered the kindness of my friend David lending me the wood from his olive groves in a tight season of commerce. I remembered pottery shelves that formed a coffin, and a delicate wooden castle that would become an artist's tool. I remembered drinking water beneath a cypress tree and the gentle reproof of a midwife. Mostly I remembered the way Ruth had spoken to me after seeing my first attempt, offering her honest consideration, and inspiring me to do more, to do my best work. Slowly, a peace came over me. Of course, Ruth was right again. My heart leapt with gratitude that she had helped me see what I should do. For what might I have felt if I had come to this stable and seen this child lying in my first attempt? I shut my eyes against the thought.

When I opened them, David the olive farmer had eased way into the small crowd, and stood just ahead of me. We watched as, one by one, people approached the manger to lay gifts near the foot of the child's bed. I saw my friend look at empty hands, then cast a searching look back over those gathered around. Again he looked back at the manger, this time his eyes glistening as though he held back tears, whether of joy or sadness I could not tell.

The news of his orchard fire had reached to all of Bethlehem. I patted Ruth's hand, then moved to David's side. "I am sorry about your orchard, my friend."

"It will be all right," he said bravely. "My heart is full." But I saw him clench empty hands, as if wishing he had something to present at the manger.

My friend sighed and pulled his wife close. With a secretive smile I inclined nearer to him and whispered, "The wood I borrowed was to build the manger in which the child lies."

David's head jerked toward me, surprise large in his eyes. He mouthed several silent, indecipherable words. Then a splendid grin spread over his whole face. As he turned to whisper the news to his wife, I stepped back beside Ruth and took her hand. Shortly, David's daughter, Elizabeth, arrived carrying a small branch. Together, they placed it at the foot of the manger, hugged, and stepped back.

As we watched in silence, a crippled man crawled toward the child. After a brief pause, he tucked his legs under him and looked directly down on the babe. I saw him speak with a man kneeling near the feedbox I'd built. A moment later, the man settled back on a bed of hay and the cripple wrapped powerful arms around the sides of the manger. I knew instantly who he was.

Other faces were familiar to me. Standing in their company, and all of us attendant to the beautiful child, I felt a quiet within, a sureness, I had never known.

A familiar voice interrupted the moment with a reverent whisper: "When would you like to start on the inn?"

Looking in at my new assistant whose arms held the child's bed fast, I pulled Ruth close, and together we thanked the babe lying in my manger.